between friends

craft projects to share

(-ăt), a. Formed of rays diverging from a center; belonging to the *Radiata* or invertebrate animals having the parts arranged radially as starfishes. — **Ra'di-a'tion**, n. — **Ra'di-a'tor**, n. That which radiates; apparatus for diffusing

ad'i-cal (răd'ĭ taining to the original; en — n. A prim rived, word; one who adv ernment. — R ness, n. — R ad'i-cel (răd' ad'i-cle (răd'ĭ becomes the r a'di-o-ac'tiv of becoming l like. a'di-o-graph ad'ish (răd'ĭ gent root eate a'di-um (rā'ĭ element. a'di-us (rā'dĭ a circle; exte forearm. a'dix (rā'dĭk word; radica af'fle (răf'f'l) tery. aft (råft), n. planks, etc. aft'er (råft'ĕr ag (răg), n. ' tatter; bit; age (rāj), n. thing eagerly rious with an ag'ged (răg'g tatters; dres ail (rāl), n. al; bar of iro cars roll; pla — v. t. To inclose with rails. — **Rail'ing**, n. Series of rails; fence. all (rāl), n. American and European game bird.

tire; banter.

Rail'road' (rāl'rōd'), **Rail'way'** (-wā'), Road with iron rails, for wheeled vehic to run on.

Rai'ment (rā'ment), n. Clothing; garmen

Rain (rān), n. Water falling from the clo in drops. — v. i. To fall in drops, or d s. — v. t.

Rain'bow', e colors of tion and ref rops of fall fe to; creat rise; lift; gi grape. native prin for collect rge surface, v. t. To scra across; e earch close an; libertin rom a perp taircase, shi ollect in ord . A rallyi banter; mo y. heep kind; battering; nger of a c press, etc m; compact walk, ride roam; wand ss-cloth pla grass; rhea. To divide i fi-ca'tion, that rams. us a

stem or root; branchy.

Ramp (rămp), v. i. To spring; frolic; romp. — n. Leap; bound. — **Ramp'age**, n. Violent behavior; excitement or passion. — **Ramp'an-cy**, n.

Ram'part (răm'pärt), n. De-

between friends

craft projects to share

CHARLOTTE LYONS

PHOTOGRAPHS BY STEVEN RANDAZZO

SIMON & SCHUSTER

New York London Toronto Sydney Singapore

Acknowledgments

Special thanks and appreciation to those who helped to make this wish come true: Robin Winge for her vision, talent, and dedication as a designer, style coach, and true friend; her assistant, Steve Wildi; Steven Randazzo for his lovely photography and easygoing style; his assistant, Nick Carbonara; Kathy Brooks for her endless offerings of quilting expertise and perpetual cheer; Colleen Mohyde for her guidance and great enthusiasm; David Rosenthal, Constance Herndon, Amanda Murray, Ginger Barton, Christine Greene, Nancy Fann, Jonathon Brodman, and Peter McCulloch for the great pleasure of this project and for all your assistance throughout; Marie Trader, Glenée von Eschen, Suzanne Hart, Barbara Coccioletti, Janet Williams, Donna Seife, Lisa Jordan, Jane Carroll, Elizabeth Sperling, Barbara Wright, Jane Berger, Debbie Resnick, Betsy Lyons Racette, Maria Kashkin, Audrey Becker, Kira and Ivan Shepherd, Wendy and Julian Perry, Kathy Gillespie, Audrey Caringella, and Ruth Hecox O'Byrne for their contributed stories, lovely faces, and borrowed homes; Rosie O'Donnell, for her enthusiastic support; Lucille Grippo at Waverly Fabrics; Michael Dinges, Nicki Dwyer, Jill Perth, Anne and Jeff O'Connor, Nan Morris, Dede Thompson, Nancy Drew, Elaine Kennelly, the Quilting Group, and my dog-walking pals. Thank you all for your encouraging words. And especially, thank you to my daughters, Erin, Maggie, and Mo, who have grown up to be the dearest girlfriends; my husband, Andy, whose support, wisdom, and culinary genius have inspired so much; and my parents, Charlotte O'Keefe and Bob Matthews.

SIMON & SCHUSTER
Rockefeller Center
1230 Avenue of the Americas
New York, NY 10020

Copyright © 2002 by Charlotte Lyons
Photography © 2002 by Steven Randazzo

For information about special discounts for bulk purchases, please contact Simon & Schuster Special Sales: 1-800-456-6798 or business@simonandschuster.com

Designed by Robin Winge, Winge & Associates, Inc., Chicago

Manufactured in the United States of America

10 9 8 7 6 5 4 3 2 1

Library of Congress Cataloging-in-Publication Data

Lyons, Charlotte.
    Between friends : craft projects to share / Charlotte Lyons; photographs by Steven Randazzo.
    p. cm.
    1. Handicraft. 2. Female friendship—Miscellanea. 3. Handicraft for girls. I. Title.
TT157.L9697 2002
745.5—dc21   2002017559

    ISBN 0-7432-1409-9

For my delightful girlfriends,
who have generously shared
so much inspiration, skill, wisdom,
humor, affection, and support.
I am fortunate to have you
each in my life.

contents

introduction

We moved to Chicago when my daughters were very young. It was summertime and the schools hadn't opened yet. Sadly, there seemed to be very few people or playmates about. On a walk one day, we spied a few children playing on the sidewalk a block away. Like parched desert travelers, we raced to the spot.

The Bridge of Oml-sea. 楢唐之田湖 (江江)

THERE ARE PEOPLE WHOM ONE LOVES IMMEDIATELY
AND FOR EVER. EVEN TO KNOW THEY ARE ALIVE IN THE WORLD
WITH ONE IS QUITE ENOUGH.

— NANCY SPAIN —

Catching up to them, we experienced an awkward moment of polite greetings as every-one sized each other up. The children quickly returned to drawing on the concrete with chubby candy-colored sticks of chalk. My take-charge daughter, Maggie, barely three years old, noticed that the two mothers were sitting on the edge of the steps, sewing and chatting. She marched over to one of the women and then bent over to her, loudly whispering, "My mom does that too. Will you talk to her so we can play with your little kids?"

That is how I met Nan, one of my best and dearest friends.

We went on to form an evening group of women who liked to sew, knit, quilt, and cross-stitch. More than anything, we liked to talk and share each other's company. Getting together was a gift in itself, and many of us would not have had the time to pursue our creative projects if not for these regular meetings. The wisdom and friendship that flew from our needles were often more beautifully crafted than the project.

We shared techniques in knitting, nurturing, quilting, coping, cooking, entertaining; we stitched and we bitched, we laughed, learned, and lifted each other over the hurdles of everyday life. Fifteen years later the group still meets once every two weeks.

I knew when I later moved to New York that if I could start or locate a group like that again, I wouldn't need Maggie to go out and find a friend for me. While I continued to nurture my old friendships from afar with small tokens of handcrafted affection, I built new friendships the same way. A handmade gift as a hostess present, party favors for a birthday luncheon—these gestures speak volumes about the importance of even the smallest offering. It wasn't long before new friends were asking, "How did you make that? Would you teach me?" I have just recently been invited into a group of women who meet monthly to sew and visit. Settled, at last.

THERE ARE NO LITTLE THINGS. "LITTLE THINGS,"
SO CALLED, ARE THE HINGES OF THE UNIVERSE.

— FANNY FERN —

Between Friends explores the bond that exists between women as friends—a bond that is richly intensified by creative endeavor. Whether a project is made for a friend or with a friend, the joy in doing so gives resonance and inspiration to an ordinary hour, day, or weekend. Little Maggie, now in college, recently called home to tell us all about a discarded crate she found in her dorm. She and her roommate spent the better part of a weekend découpaging it for their room. Her excitement was all wound up with the fun they had sharing the project, their pride in their inventive cleverness, and the enviable finished product. They were going to show the girls at the end of the hall how to make one too. The circle widens.

Between raising children and working a job, women have learned to set aside a little leisure time for their interests. Increasingly, women of all ages are turning their creativity toward home and hobby, discovering that découpaging a box, knitting a tea cozy, stitching a quilt, or embroidering a pillow can be a restful,

fulfilling activity. At the same time, the idea of "home" itself has become more precious in recent years, given the dwindling amounts of time we have to enjoy ourselves there. It is no surprise that the personal ways in which we enhance our homes give strength to the very real comfort they offer. This sentiment dovetails precisely with a woman's approach to friendship: Celebrate and personalize the bonds of friendship with creativity and enthusiasm.

Between Friends offers a wide selection of craft activities to share with a friend or a group of friends. The projects are fun to do, easy to make, and lovely enough to inspire those with a budding creative curiosity or a lifetime of expertise. Most are excellent gift ideas you can create for a friend, who will treasure your thoughtfulness, the unique gift of yourself, as well as the delightful finished piece. Better still, the materials needed are often those found right inside the pantry or craft basket. So get out your page markers, call up your adventurous friends, and let the fun begin!

HAPPINESS IS A BY-PRODUCT OF AN EFFORT
TO MAKE SOMEONE ELSE HAPPY.
— GRETTA BROOKER PALMER —

PAPERWEIGHTS

SEED PACKETS

BERRY BASKET

in an hour

I have always loved to make gifts for my friends. For a while I seemed to be the only one who did that, and sometimes I thought maybe I should go shopping, like everyone else. But now that I have friends who make beautiful presents also, I know how much a handmade gift is cherished. I am forever tied to each one, knowing that it is thoroughly unique, that it is full of my friend's heart and soul, and that she chose me to be the delighted recipient. She made it for me!

WRITE IT ON YOUR HEART THAT EVERY DAY
IS THE BEST DAY OF THE YEAR.

— RALPH WALDO EMERSON —

PAINTED TEAPOT

PAGE

24

HONEY BISCUITS

PAGE

26

QUICK FRAME

PAGE

28

DÉCOUPAGED VASES

PAGE 32

personal touch is what makes your effort so dearly prized in the end. Take a chance, step out of the instructions, and discover your talents.

If you have a group of friends to join forces with, a project like *Paperweights* or *Place Card Holders* is perfect for a casual gathering. Get the materials together and ask the

SCISSORS KEEPER

PAGE 36

A handmade project doesn't have to take very long. An hour is plenty of time to make all sorts of things with simple materials. The projects in this chapter are quick and easy, but they have style that will say as much about your personality as your skill. Experiment with the materials at hand and customize the design to reflect who you are. Certainly the

PLACE CARDS

PAGE 34

girls over. You will be amazed at the different interpretations that emerge from the same design, not to mention the fun that everyone will have working together. You might want to number the finished pieces and draw to see who gets whose. No matter what, everyone goes home smiling, creatively inspired and gifted with a party favor.

paperweights

Having placed a few favorite buttons and charms inside a small glass dish on my desk, I found that they were fun to swirl around while talking on the phone. They reminded me of dimestore toys with loose beads that fall into grooves to make a picture. Turning the dish upside down, I realized that with a bottom, it could be a mini shadow box. A set of small crystal ashtrays from a thrift shop became perfect showcases for solitary objects, like a butterfly wing and a heart-shaped rock. If you aren't the thrift shop hound that some of us are, look for

IF YOU KEEP A THING FOR SEVEN YEARS,
YOU ARE SURE TO FIND A USE FOR IT.

— SIR WALTER SCOTT —

glass coasters or ashtrays from department stores. This project makes an unusual personal gift or perhaps a party favor. Better still, make a set of place cards by writing each guest's name inside on the base so that your guests have to scramble the contents to find theirs. What a clever way to make the most of a few stray buttons and a scrap of pretty paper.

BEGIN BY PLACING the dish over your selection of objects and checking to make sure that they can move about freely inside the dome of the inverted glass. Choose a paper background and trace around the dish. Cut out the paper background and repeat the process for a matching cardboard back. (Use the cardboard from a notepad or one that is similar in weight.)

Repeat for a felt backing that will cover the cardboard underneath and finish the back. Glue the felt to one side of the cardboard and the decorative paper to the opposite side. Set aside to dry.

Clean the dish inside. Check for fit with the dry cardboard base. Set the cardboard base with the decorative paper side up, cluster the objects in the center, and apply a rim of glue to the outermost edge of the paper.

you will need

- A SMALL GLASS DISH OR ASHTRAY WITHOUT RIM INDENTATIONS
- AN ASSORTMENT OF BUTTONS, CHARMS, AND OTHER TRINKETS
- DECORATIVE PAPER FOR BACKING
- PENCIL AND SCISSORS
- LIGHTWEIGHT CARDBOARD
- FELT FOR BACKING
- WHITE GLUE

Carefully position the inverted glass onto the base without disturbing the objects. It is important to keep the objects free of any stray glue. Weight the glass top with a can of soup or a book and allow to dry undisturbed.

seed packets

One of the nicest things about gardeners is that they are eager to share: cut flowers, plant wisdom, a cozy corner where you can sit and sip lemonade together. Perhaps best of all are shared cuttings or seeds. Late in summer I enjoy collecting seeds from my favorite, most successful plants. To pass a thimbleful of seeds along to a friend is a small but meaningful gesture that brings the promise of spring and new pleasures to come. Make these decorative labels for plain envelopes and fill them with seeds to give away, or bundle several envelopes together with a pretty ribbon as a gift for a fellow plantswoman. You may even be gifted with a return envelope that promises yet another season of surprises in the garden.

YOU DON'T HAVE A GARDEN JUST FOR YOURSELF. YOU HAVE IT TO SHARE.

— AUGUSTA CARTER —

SEEDS
FROM THE
GARDEN OF
KATHY
BROOKS

you will need

- CLIP ART OR A CLEAR COPY OF
  A GARDENING IMAGE
- A COMPUTER WITH PRINTER OR
  A BLACK PEN FOR HAND
  LETTERING
- WHITE PAPER
- PAPER CUTTER
- SPRAY ADHESIVE
- YELLOW KEY ENVELOPES, 2¹/₂" x 4¹/₄"
- RAFFIA OR RIBBON

SELECT AN IMAGE for the label that is appropriate for the size and style of your lettering. A delicate typeface will work with an old-fashioned Victorian image; a bolder style can be paired with a stronger graphic design. Try to balance the weight of the lines.

Lay out the information on the computer and arrange to fit the dimensions of the label, which should be roughly 2¹/₄ by 3³/₄ inches. Be sure to add a border for crisp definition. If you don't have a clip art image stored in your computer, you can copy one and paste it onto your label.

Carefully line the image up, then copy the whole thing for a finished page. Reduce or enlarge on the copier to attain the best fit for the envelope. Repeat the process to make enough labels to paste onto 12 key envelopes. Carefully cut them out and spray the backs with adhesive, then apply them to the front of the envelopes. Stack and tie together with raffia or a ribbon.

VARIATION ON THE PROJECT

— magnets —

Do you have a friend who loves animals—or some other special thing? Find a quote that matches her interest, like this one about dogs, and combine it with a charming image or clip art that has the same theme.

Use the same technique to print and paste the image and quote onto a piece of chipboard trimmed with fancy paper edgers.

Apply a self-adhering strip of magnet tape to the back to make a quick and easy magnet.

:: Activities and Suggestions for a Garden Club ::

ADOPT a school side yard and get together with students and teachers to help them learn about gardening. Beautify and teach at the same time.

PAINT clay pots and fill with small seedlings for Arbor Day. Give them away at a town function.

ORGANIZE a tour of local gardens to raise money for a charity.

PUBLISH a handbook of tips for natural pesticide-free gardening.

DEVELOP recipes for edible plants that you can grow at home. Have everyone over for a potluck test kitchen.

FIND a secondhand garden bench or birdbath. Make it over with paint and imagination, then install it in a town park or hospital green space.

LEARN to appliqué and translate your love of flowers into a quilt square. Then combine the various member squares into a larger quilt to auction for charity or

hang at an open house to interest new members.

INVITE a watercolorist to the meeting to teach members how to paint their gardens in bloom.

DECORATE store-bought straw hats for sun protection. Collect hats, paint, ribbons, and other decorations. At a meeting, have a table set up with everything needed so that members can get right to work. The same idea also works for garden totes or smocks.

GARDEN CLUB

Backyard Leaves 10.16.00

berry basket

There is something about a strawberry basket that makes it very hard to pitch. The handy shape is eminently useful, and the basketry weave has inspired thousands of crafty makeovers. Here's one more reinvention—slipcover it with some gift wrap scraps for a disguise that is absolute. Fill it with frosted cookies for a friend or with welcoming bath treats and soaps for the guest room. Vary the paper covering to match the theme, and the possibilities will continue as far as your imagination reaches.

PLACE A BASKET side flat against a plain piece of paper and trace its shape. Repeat for the basket front. Cut out these two patterns and use as templates. On the back of a piece of gift wrap, place a template so that it can be traced twice, with a mirror image of the same shape connected along the top edge. This way you can fold the paper in half and drop it onto the basket side so that the fold covers the basket rim. You will need two sides and a front and back created this way. Trace around the basket bottom on the gift wrap and cut out this piece. Thread a needle with a length of sturdy raffia.

Drop one panel onto one side and lace the top edge with a whip stitch, using the basket as a grid, poking the needle through the paper and the open holes in the basket. When you get to the corner, add another panel and continue until you have laced the four panels to the basket all along the top edge. Use the same technique to lace the side edges at the corners from top to bottom. When complete, drop in the bottom piece, decorative side up. If desired, lace around the bottom edges of paper and basket. Fill the basket with excelsior straw or another loose filling of your choice. Add treats as planned.

you will need

- A CLEAN AND DRY BERRY BASKET
- PLAIN PAPER
- PENCIL AND SCISSORS
- GIFT WRAP OR DECORATIVE PAPER PIECES LARGE ENOUGH TO COVER THE FOUR SIDES INSIDE AND OUT AND THE BOTTOM INSIDE
- RAFFIA AND A LARGE-EYED NEEDLE

painted teapot

I f you have ever moved into a new neighborhood, surely you remember that day when you thought, "Oh, dear, what did I do? Where in the world am I?" This project could be the life-saver you toss to rescue a newcomer in your neighborhood who is suffering pangs of regret and the total exhaustion of a move. A department store teapot or even one from a thrift shop (I find plain white ones in almost every shop I enter) can be changed in just a few minutes. This idea came to me when I found a pair of teacups from a Chinese take-out restaurant that

had the restaurant telephone number printed on the side. I thought what a good marketing tool—for a restaurant or a new friend. No need to look the number up; it is easily in view whenever the thought arises for tea and company.

WASH AND DRY the teapot. Practice stamping first on a piece of newspaper to develop a technique that you are comfortable with. Pick out the rubber stamp letters that spell your name and telephone number, then use a foam brush to apply a scant amount of paint to each stamp before applying it to the side of the teapot. Fill the remaining area with a neutral character, such as a hyphen, period, or decorative image.

Place in a cool oven and bake according to the paint manufacturer's directions.

you will need

- A PLAIN WHITE CHINA TEAPOT
- RUBBER STAMPS IN AN ALPHABET WITH NUMERALS
- NEWSPAPER
- ACRYLIC PERMANENT PAINTS
- A FOAM BRUSH
- AN OVEN IN WHICH TO BAKE THE FINISHED TEAPOT

honey biscuits

When a friend comes over for coffee, surprise her with these pretty biscuits made from pantry biscuit mix rolled and cut in a novel way. They look like a lot more fuss than they really are.

PREHEAT THE OVEN to 400°F. Combine the biscuit mix with the milk in a large bowl. Remove and knead the dough for 10 strokes, then roll out on a lightly floured board into a rectangle roughly 8 by 15 inches. Brush with the butter and honey mixture. Sprinkle with the cinnamon sugar mixture. Cut in half widthwise. Cut one half into 5 strips about 1 1/2 inches wide. Stack the 5 strips and repeat for the remaining half. Trim the rough ends and cut each stack into 4 equal pieces.

Lightly spray the mini muffin tin with cooking spray. Slightly pinch one end of each piece of

you will need

- 2 1/4 CUPS DRY BISCUIT MIX
- 2/3 CUP MILK
- 2 TABLESPOONS MELTED BUTTER COMBINED WITH 1 TABLESPOON HONEY
- 3 TABLESPOONS SUGAR COMBINED WITH 1 1/4 TEASPOONS CINNAMON
- ROLLING PIN AND MINI MUFFIN TIN WITH EIGHT 2" MUFFIN CUPS

stacked dough before you place it in the cup, pinched end down. While baking, the top part of the stack will flare out like a flower. Bake for 18 minutes. Remove and serve while warm.

Makes 8 biscuits.

FRIENDSHIP IS THE BREAD OF THE HEART.

— MARY RUSSELL MITFORD —

quick frame

Rummaging through a keepsake box or scrapbook, you are bound to come across an old snapshot or two that brings on a wave of nostalgia—and a smile to go with it. Perhaps it's a forgotten picture of you and an old friend huddled together in a fit of giggles, your dress-up outfits and tiaras aglow. Make a quick frame for a simple snapshot or photocopy of the original, and send it off to your friend as a big greeting card. Rustic but charming, this casual presentation will bring back that youthful sparkle. So easy to make, it could also serve as a darling invitation, with the party information printed on a removable card for the calendar.

THE PAST IS PERPETUAL YOUTH TO THE HEART.
— L. E. LANDON —

as a homing pigeon. More birds might come ___ of them n___ ady Peggy

perch an___ red the bar___ Lady Peggy ___ rushed into the barn and took___ aper fastened to her pi___ more exciting than get___

She u___ and read:

Your f___ ty-pound fish today. I___ ging the word because ___ "ladies first." I will co___

Percival

And that is how Clara Parker, before the days of airplanes and radio, got a message by pigeon air mail.

piece of paper slightly smaller than the photo to use as a template. Trace around it on the frame front to mark the photo's placement and cutting lines. Open the folded cardboard and use the box cutter and cutting mat to cut an opening slightly smaller than the photo template. Place the photo inside and check to see that it fits the opening. Set the photo aside and cover the front of the frame with decorative paper or fabric.

SCORE BUT DO NOT CUT through the cardboard across the middle so that it will fold in half, like a card. Keeping the hinge at the bottom (or the top if you are making a standing frame), fold the scored cardboard in half. Cut a

Cut the paper or fabric to fit and spray the back with adhesive. Apply to the front of the frame. To finish, place the photo inside, fold and close the frame, and lay it flat on a length of ribbon. Wrap the ribbon from the back to the front and tie a bow, as shown. Use two straight pins to pierce the ribbon and the cardboard at each side. Hang from the ribbon back.

you will need

- A PIECE OF CORRUGATED CARDBOARD 5" x 14" FOR A 5" x 7" FINISHED FRAME
- PLAIN PAPER AND PENCIL
- A BOX CUTTER
- CUTTING MAT
- PHOTO TO BE FRAMED
- DECORATIVE PAPER OR FABRIC
- SPRAY ADHESIVE OR GLUE STICK
- RIBBON (24" TO 36" IN LENGTH)
- 2 STRAIGHT PINS

E rin is my oldest. Perhaps because handmade things have always taken center stage at our family occasions, she makes gifts for her friends too. "I realized early on that the handmade gifts with more sentimental value lasted longer. I still have all the things everyone made for me. Whenever I have to give a gift, I consider making it myself first.

Between Friends: Erin and Maya, Kari and Jessye

"In junior high my friends and I made these collage cards to give to one another —huge, poster-sized cards collaged with cutouts. That led to more well-crafted gifts, like the photo album Maya made for me senior year. I still have that too."

Maya and Erin went to the university together where they met Kari, who shared their appreciation of art. "Kari liked to paint and decorate furniture with lines of original poetry or quotes. When she told me that she had painted her car with a girlfriend, covering the whole thing with fish, I thought that was so cool. And she was interested in all the projects we did at our house. Since college, each of us has moved into larger crafts. Maya makes batiks, Kari has gone into furniture design, and I am experimenting with bookbinding and

printmaking. Recently Kari gave me a knitted scarf for Christmas. She chose the color for me, and even though it was her first project, she had me in mind for it all along. I wear it with pride, knowing that the charm is that it isn't store-bought but is trendy all the same. She missed a bunch of stitches, but that is a constant reminder of the homemade-ness. If it were perfect, no one would ask me if I made it and then I wouldn't be able to talk about Kari."

After college, when Erin moved to Chicago, she met Jessye at work. Erin explains that again the arts provided a stepping stone for friendship: "In one of our first conversations, we talked about a particular T. S. Eliot poem we both loved and a stanza she told me contained her favorite lines. The words were buzzing around in my

head at a printmaking workshop, so I used the lines in my print. As soon as I saw how well it turned out, I knew I would give it to her, even though we were just beginning to be friends. It was Christmas, but it seemed too big a gift for such a new acquaintance, so I wrapped it casually, not to seem too elaborate. On my day off, I took it to work and pulled her aside. When she opened it, she got all flushed and I could tell she was going to cry, and I started getting a little emotional too. Then we hugged, she said thank you, and we've been good friends ever since. She had me over for a dinner party and pointed out the prominent spot where she had hung the print. It's a little ironic that the lines of the poem are about loneliness and our ineptitude at connecting with one another."

découpaged vases

Make a simple bouquet a keepsake gift with a Matisse-y découpaged glass container. Start by looking in the basement for those flower shop vases that you couldn't help but save, or go to the thrift shop, where they are cheap enough for you to treat yourself to a variety of pretty shapes and sizes, but avoid those with rough, bumpy surfaces. Whether you are creating a centerpiece for a party, taking a gift to a friend, or looking for a project to share, this is a foolproof way to experiment with a playful sense of design and your own inventive style.

TEAR THE COLORED TISSUE into small pieces. Paint the backs of the tissue pieces with glue and stick them onto the glass vase, smoothing out the bubbles and pressing down the edges. Wrinkles are pretty much unavoidable with this technique and add nice texture and dimension to the tissue layer. Cover the entire vase in this way. With a contrasting colored paper, such as a crisp origami sheet, cut out free-form shapes and designs of your own choosing to decorate the tissue-covered vase.

Experiment with different patterns and shapes, such as leaves or flowers. Draw the shapes on the back of the colored paper and cut them out. Paint the backs with glue and stick them onto the vase, smoothing out bubbles and pressing down edges again. Cut inch-wide strips of paper and then cut them in half lengthwise with a scalloped or zigzagged edge. Use the strips as vertical borders. When the paper is thoroughly dry, cover with two coats of acrylic satin varnish.

you will need

- COLORED TISSUE PAPER
- FOAM BRUSHES
- WHITE GLUE OR DÉCOUPAGE MEDIUM
- A CLEAN GLASS VASE WITH A SMOOTH, UNTEXTURED SURFACE
- CONTRASTING COLORED COPY PAPER, ORIGAMI PAPER, OR DECORATIVE PAPER OF YOUR CHOICE
- SCISSORS
- ACRYLIC SATIN VARNISH

place cards

A celebration at the table becomes a great deal more with the addition of place cards. Almost anyone loves to see her name written on a card, especially in a personal style, on a festive occasion. These place card holders are so much fun to make that your guests will want to stay after lunch and pick your brain to learn how you made them. Why not get the junk bag out, make another pot of coffee, and let everyone have a turn?

SPRAY-PAINT the bottle caps inside and out. Allow to dry. Cut out a plug of Styrofoam that is slightly larger than a cap. Cut a length of wire approximately 15 inches long. Bend the wire into a double ring with the two ends meeting. Set the cap on the table like a cup and hold the double ring of wire against it vertically, with the two ends at the bottom. Place the Styrofoam plug inside the double ring, right over the two ends, and force it down into the cap so that the plug secures the ends of the wire inside, against the bottom of the cap.

Use a glue gun to glue moss or fabric to the top of the Styrofoam plug to conceal it. Then glue on a pleasing combination of trinkets, beads, or buttons.

When finished, slide a decorative place card between the two loops near the top.

you will need

- GOLD SPRAY PAINT
- CAPS FROM BOTTLES, SUCH AS SPICES, VITAMINS, BLEACH, OR DRINKS, 1 1/2" IN DIAMETER AND WITH A 1/2" TO 3/4" RIM
- STYROFOAM
- 18-GAUGE STEEL WIRE
- WIRE SNIPS
- HOT GLUE GUN
- DRIED MOSS OR FABRIC
- TRINKETS, BEADS, OR BUTTONS

scissors keeper

The members of my sewing group exchange gifts around the holidays—just a little something, such as a small sewing-related trinket to drop into the sewing basket or knitting bag. One year I made little scissors keepers for everyone, knowing how much I enjoy the one I have. Made from wool felt and simply decorated, the tidy pocket with a snap flap keeps a pair of embroidery snips neatly tucked away, which your friends will dearly appreciate on days when it seems that few things find their way back to their rightful places.

ENLARGE THE PATTERN on page 154. Transfer the pattern to the felt and cut out

a back piece and a front. Line up the edges and pin the front to the back. Beginning at the top of one front edge, blanket-stitch the two pieces together all along the sides and bottom. Continue the blanket stitch along the raw edge of the top flap. Knot securely and clip the thread. Sew the two snap parts in place on the pocket front and the corresponding inside of the top flap. Cut out a flower from the scrap felt and a flower center of a different color. Cut out a leaf sprig. Tack the leaves and flower securely in place on the front of the flap.

you will need

- TRACING PAPER AND PENCIL
- A 10" x 10" PIECE OF WOOL OR CRAFT FELT
- SCISSORS
- STRAIGHT PINS
- PEARL COTTON AND NEEDLE
- A SNAP OR VELCRO BUTTON
- SMALL SCRAPS OF FELT IN COMPLEMENTARY COLORS FOR THE FLOWER AND LEAVES

NOTE BOX

BOOK BAG

FLEA MARKET PILLOW

half a day

A half day or an evening of leisure time with friends is a delicious luxury. Book club, sewing group, girls night out, or flea market raiders—all are opportunities to indulge our girl-ness and to celebrate the friendships that we have built through a network of interests. Whatever the occasion, this is the fun we live for. The projects in this chapter are meant to be shared with girlfriends as gifts or as group activities that can be explored together.

IN MY FRIEND I FIND A SECOND SELF.

— ISABEL NORTON —

38

ORGANIZER

PAGE

50

OATMEAL CAKE

PAGE

54

OCCASION PLATE

PAGE

56

BASKET SACHETS

PAGE 60

mâché in the backyard while the kids play. Use an afternoon on your own to fluff up the guest room for an old roommate's upcoming visit or découpage a gift plate for a bridal shower. Dig through your scrap basket and craft closet for an inventory of ideas and materials.

POTATO PRINT BOX

PAGE 64

Take off with the girls to scour the flea market or tag sales for vintage textiles to use in home-decorating projects. Pack up the materials for the sachet project and cart them off to your sewing group. Perhaps a friend there can give you tips for making ribbon flowers. Invite a neighbor over to experiment with papier-

A treasured button might seem just the thing for a hand-sewn pillow, a decoration on a papier-mâché box, or the center of a felt flower. Whatever you do, put your heart into it and share that happy thrill with your friends. Your thoughtful intentions and infectious enthusiasm make all things possible.

Have you ever wanted to try your hand at papier-mâché or découpage but thought you would need all sorts of fancy equipment? Look no further than the kitchen pantry. For the most part, all you need should be right there. Well, you might have to make some brownies first because this project calls for an empty brownie mix carton. Just cut it  down into an interesting shape in front and trim the back, then cover it with papier-mâché so that no one else will know …until you tell them (which you will because it will be such an

THE BEST THINGS IN LIFE ARE FREE.
— ANONYMOUS —

40

FRIENDSHIP

Friendship is the sun breaking through a cloud; it is the fragrance of a flower released when the bud bursts into bloom; it is the twinkling of myriad stars in the night sky; it is the voice of God in the heart.

E. M. Brainerd

amazing thing that you did). Here is a chance to experiment with new craft techniques and end up with a useful note box or wall pocket to give to a friend or keep for yourself. Maybe make two.

BEGIN BY TRIMMING the box to a shape like the one pictured. First, cut off the boxtop. Leaving the back uncut, use the scissors to cut down the sides and front so that 5 inches of box remain on these three sides. Draw (try using a saucer as a template) and then cut a V-shaped notch in the front, making an interesting center point. On the back, draw an appealing shape and then cut that out too.

you will need

- A BROWNIE CARTON OR SOME OTHER SUITABLY SHAPED CARDBOARD CARTON OR BOX
- SCISSORS
- PUSHPIN
- A SHORT PIECE OF WIRE
- MASKING TAPE
- FLOUR
- WHITE GLUE
- TORN NEWSPAPER STRIPS, 1" x 6"
- WHITE ACRYLIC PAINT
- FOAM BRUSHES
- MAGAZINE OR CATALOG CUTOUTS AND DECORATIVE PAPER
- DÉCOUPAGE MEDIUM OR WHITE GLUE
- ACRYLIC SATIN VARNISH
- PEARLY BUTTON

Use a pushpin to make two holes in the back, 2 inches from the top and 1 inch apart. Fish the wire through both holes to make a hanging loop on the back. Twist on the front of the box and cover the twist with a piece of masking tape.

Mix papier-mâché paste in a small bowl: 1 cup warm water, 1/2 cup flour, and 1 tablespoon white glue. Dip the newspaper strips in the paste and run between your fingers to remove excess paste. Apply the wet strips to the box, covering all surfaces and edges with a single layer. Allow to dry completely. Repeat for a second layer and be sure to cover the bottom also. Rough edges can be sanded. After the box is dry, apply a base of white acrylic. Allow to dry.

To découpage, cut pieces of decorative paper to fit the sides, back, and front in a pleasing collage of patterns and colors. Try combining stripes with printed patterns or garden images. Old letters and copies of photographs work very well. Look in magazines and catalogs for possibilities to mix and match. Coat the backs of these with glue or découpage medium and apply to the dry papier-mâché surfaces, being sure

to press out bubbles and wrinkles as much as possible. Don't forget to paper the inside too.

When finished, apply two coats of acrylic satin varnish. Decorate the front with a pearly button glued in place. Hang or stand and fill with note cards.

book bag

L ike so many wonderful things in our lives, books are meant to be shared—not just literally, but also intellectually. Recommendations for good books can be passed across the garden gate or more officially in a book club. Reading and sharing the same book are friendly ways to exchange ideas and feelings about all sorts of things. This book bag keeps your titles ready to go—whether back to the library or off to a meeting.

FRIENDS, BOOKS, A CHEERFUL HEART,
AND CONSCIENCE CLEAR
ARE THE MOST CHOICE COMPANIONS WE HAVE HERE.

— WILLIAM MATHER —

green felt, pinning them onto the basket top as you go. Stitch in place with white thread. Place the blue decorated panel 3 inches from the bottom of one gingham rectangle. Zigzag or blanket-stitch securely in place. With right sides together, stitch the two gingham rectangles together. Fold down the top hem 2 inches and stitch. At the bottom, fold up the side corners inside the bag 1 inch and stitch to the side seam so that the bottom will have a flat gusset. Turn and press.

Cut a strip of gingham 4 by 28 inches long. Fold in half lengthwise and sew down the long edge. Turn and press. Pin and stitch securely to the bag sides at the top.

you will need

- SCISSORS AND STRAIGHT PINS
- 1/2 YARD OF MEDIUM-WEIGHT COT-TON FABRIC, SUCH AS THE GING-HAM USED HERE
- 7" x 9 1/2" OF BLUE COTTON FABRIC OR ANOTHER CONTRASTING COLOR
- SEWING THREAD
- SEWING MACHINE
- A SCRAP OF RIBBON OR FABRIC (USED FOR THE BASKET-BOTTOM DECORATION)
- GREEN AND WHITE FELT SCRAPS AND 4 RED BUTTONS

IF YOU PREFER, use a ready-made canvas bag and copy the basket design (page 152) to decorate it. To make your own bag, cut two pieces of cotton, 11 by 16 inches. Set aside. Cut a rectangle, 7 by 9 1/2 inches, of blue cotton for the basket background. Cut the basket shape out of the small gingham print and pin it to the blue rectangle, 1 1/2 inches from the bottom center. Fold down the top of the basket 3/4 inch and stitch in place using a machine zigzag stitch or a blanket stitch by hand. Add a contrasting band cut from ribbon at the bottom of the basket if desired.

Cut four flower shapes from white felt to fit the four red buttons you have selected to use as flower centers. Cut stems and leaves from the

:: Activities and Suggestions for a Book Club ::

DESIGN a bookplate for club members, as in the *Seed Packet* project in Chapter One. Have them printed at a copy shop.

HAVE a costume party and ask everyone to come as a favorite fictional character.

COOK a theme meal inspired by a recently studied book. Read *Memoirs of a Geisha?* Create a menu based on Japanese foods and culture.

ORGANIZE a book sale for your library.

MAKE a journal cover for book club notes and calendar.

STITCH a bedside reader case that hangs from the side of the bed, providing a place to store books.

COLLECT beads and charms that can be fashioned into bookmarks. Stitch a felt or fabric strip, then sew the decorative beads onto one end.

FILL a gift basket with titles that your group has enjoyed and donate it to a hospital. At a senior center, have each member adopt a partner and grow a book club there.

GO to a flea market and collect curios and collectibles to turn into one-of-a-kind bookends. Glue your treasures to standard office bookends.

BOOK CLUB

flea market pillow

Needlepoint is an intensive craft. These small works are to be admired, along with the unknown women who managed such tedious bits of stitchery. Occasionally I will find one at a tag sale, unfinished and waiting for a stage to star on. Matched up with a handful of coordinating fabrics, a little needlepoint can carry on as a prominent pillow decoration. This same idea also works nicely for an embroidered tea towel, bits of lavish trim, quilt patches, or even a crocheted potholder.

INSPECT THE WORK for any damage that might require mending. Determine the best part of the work and measure the dimensions of this section. Plan the placement on the pillow front accordingly. Cut four strips from the fabric that will frame it—allowing for hemming at each side. (Example: A finished frame strip of 2 inches should be cut 2 3/4 inches to allow for a 3/8-inch seam allowance on each side.) The top and bottom strips must be longer to accommodate the increased width of the work after the two side strip additions. With right sides together, pin the right and left sides of the fabric strip to the needlepoint. Fold back to check for correct placement. Adjust if necessary and machine-sew through both layers on both sides. Open and press lightly. Pin the top and bottom strips across the needlepoint and side strips. Open again, check for correct placement and to be sure the design is square. Stitch. Trim to equal widths on all four strip sashes and fold under 3/8 inch for the hem. Press. Pin and blind-stitch the framed needlepoint to the center of the pillow.

you will need

- A NEEDLEPOINT IN GOOD CONDITION, OR SOME OTHER TEXTILE
- A PILLOW COVERED IN A MATCHING FABRIC
- 1/4 YARD FABRIC TO COORDINATE WITH BOTH THE PILLOW AND THE NEEDLEPOINT
- SCISSORS AND STRAIGHT PINS
- SEWING MACHINE
- MASKING TAPE

Secondhand linen stands at flea markets and tag sales are magnets for women who find their dainty yet sturdy snippets of the past irresistible. The look and feeling of vintage handwork inspire nostalgia in anyone who appreciates the delicacy of intricate needle-work. It's dizzying to think that women even embroidered cocktail napkins and then washed and ironed them too! These little linens are bound to be the most overlooked and underpriced offerings on the table, so scoop them up for a song and take

HAPPINESS IS A PERFUME YOU CANNOT POUR ON OTHERS
WITHOUT GETTING A FEW DROPS ON YOURSELF.

— ANONYMOUS —

them home to the sewing machine. Crochet-trimmed hand towels and cutwork napkins are perfect pockets for this dressing room organizer, easily stitched up to fit a hanger. Use the side openings for lingerie and the small linen pockets for jewelry, and attach favorite pins to the front. This project is perfectly suited for a guest room or bath—you won't have the heart to hang such a pretty thing in the closet.

CUT TWO RECTANGLES of fabric, 18 by 28 inches. Lay one piece, for the front of the bag, flat on a table, right side up. Pin each decorative linen napkin in place as desired for a pocket, allowing one edge to fold down to make a pretty pocket flap that shows off the stitchery or a monogram. A hand towel should be large enough to use as a double pocket; fold the bottom up by two-thirds for a second pocket. Machine- or hand-stitch the linens in place.

Place the back piece over the front so that the two fabric pieces are right sides together on the table. Place a hanger at the top and trace the shape of the hanger onto the wrong side of one piece of the fabric. Mark an opening for the hanger top. Pin all along this new silhouette.

Sew the front and back together along the top except where you've marked the opening for the hanger. Sew 3 inches down each side. Stop and leave 8 inches open on each side, then continue sewing down each side and across the bottom.

Turn, press, and blind-stitch the edges of the side pocket openings and the hanger opening at the top, leaving them open. Insert the hanger through a side opening and the top hanger opening and check for fit. Adjust as necessary and add lace trim along the top edge if desired, hand-stitching in place.

you will need

- 1 YARD OF DECORATOR FABRIC, 45" WIDE
- SCISSORS AND STRAIGHT PINS
- 3 COCKTAIL NAPKINS, HANDKERCHIEFS, OR HAND TOWELS
- SEWING MACHINE
- A STRONG HANGER, PREFERABLY AN OLDER WOOD ONE WITH A PRETTY TOP
- DECORATIVE LACE TRIM (OPTIONAL)

A PLACE FOR EVERYTHING AND EVERYTHING IN ITS PLACE.

— ISABELLA MARY BEETON —

oatmeal cake

Some cakes are meant to be eaten at any time of day, and this is definitely one of them. It's good for breakfast and it is perfect for coffee with friends. It is a wonderful luncheon dessert and also just right for an evening get-together. It even travels well if kept in the pan. Frankly, this yummy cake is quite fabulous all day long. Make and bring one along if you are an invited guest for a girls' weekend. You will rise to the top of the list of favorite guests.

POUR BOILING WATER over the oats in a bowl and let stand 20 minutes. Preheat the oven to 350°F. Cream the butter with both sugars and add the eggs. Sift the flour, baking soda, cinnamon, and salt together and add to the butter mixture. Mix thoroughly, then add the soaked oats. Grease the springform pan and pour in the batter. Bake for 50 minutes.

To make the frosting, melt the butter in a saucepan. Add the evaporated milk, brown sugar, and vanilla. Mix lightly. Stir in the coconut and chopped nuts. Spread over the warm cake and place under the broiler briefly, until the top is lightly browned. Cool thoroughly before removing the sides of the pan.

you will need

• A 9 1/2" SPRINGFORM PAN

CAKE:
• 1 1/2 CUPS BOILING WATER
• 1 CUP ROLLED OATS
• 1/2 CUP BUTTER
• 3/4 CUP WHITE SUGAR
• 3/4 CUP BROWN SUGAR
• 2 EGGS
• 1 1/2 CUPS FLOUR
• 1 TEASPOON BAKING SODA
• 3/4 TEASPOON CINNAMON
• 1/4 TEASPOON SALT

FROSTING:
• 1/4 CUP BUTTER
• 1/4 CUP EVAPORATED MILK
• 3/4 CUP BROWN SUGAR
• 1 TEASPOON VANILLA
• 1 CUP SHREDDED SWEETENED COCONUT
• 1 CUP CHOPPED WALNUTS OR PECANS

occasion plate

A wedding or the birth of a baby is a signature event in a woman's life. Commemorate the joy and sentiment that accompany such special occasions with this découpage and paint project. The finished work has a timeless appeal that is just right for an elegant wedding invitation or adorable birth announcement. If you have a friend whose daughter is the bride or new mother, this is the perfect present for her. After all, she is collecting milestone memories of her own.

CIRCLES, THOUGH SMALL, ARE YET COMPLETE.

— ANONYMOUS —

stray glue and allow to dry. Next, cut a ring of gold tissue and use decorative paper edgers to trim the outside edge. Paste this behind the invitation so that it shows around the interior invitation design.

To finish the baby plate, use an artist's brush and paint to make a decorative scalloped border. Paint the scallops and polka dots first, then cover with two coats of background color. To finish the wedding plate, tear pie-shaped strips of copied music or handwriting and apply like wheel spokes around the plate rim from the

TO BEGIN, choose the invitation or other image for the center of the plate and enlarge or reduce it on a copier to fit the center, flat part of the plate. (Make extras to experiment with.) Trace, cut, and decoratively trim this piece to fit. If you are adding clip art, such as the rings and bouquet on the wedding invitation, copy them on similar paper and cut them out. Use the découpage medium to paste them onto the front of the invitation before you apply the invitation to the plate back. For the baby plate, you can add the baby's name beneath the artwork with a permanent marker or calligraphy pen. You might want to practice on a few of the extra copies of the image first.

Clean the back of the glass plate. If you want a gold rim, paint one on before you begin to découpage. Use découpage medium and a foam brush to paint the front of the trimmed invitation or announcement and place it against the back of the plate so that it shows through. Use your finger to press out any bubbles between glass and paper as much as possible. Clean off

you will need

- A COPY OF THE ARTWORK OR INVITATION
- A 10" GLASS PLATE
- SHARP SCISSORS AND PAPER EDGERS
- CLIP ART IMAGES TO FIT THE OCCASION
- DÉCOUPAGE MEDIUM, SUCH AS MOD PODGE
- PERMANENT MARKER OR CALLIGRAPHY PEN
- FOAM BRUSH AND ARTIST'S BRUSHES
- COTTON SWABS
- PERMANENT ACRYLIC PAINTS
- GOLD TISSUE PAPER
- FELT FOR BACKING (OPTIONAL)

center to the outside edge, overlapping paper strips slightly as you go. When dry, trim at the plate edge. Cover the back with felt, gold tissue, or paint for a clean, protected finish. The finished plate cannot be washed but can be cleaned with glass cleaner.

Among the benefits of a girls' getaway weekend is the chance to turn new friends into old friends. The kind of bonding that takes place over a few days of intensive togetherness without the cares of day-to-day life is truly energizing. Marie was invited to a girls' weekend at a friend's lake cottage and arrived to find that Glenée was her roommate.

Between Friends: Marie and Glenée

Just like kids at summer camp, they found it hard to stay quiet after lights out—chatting and discovering that they shared common interests and bright ideas to beat the dawn. Marie was struck by Glenée's boundless, clever ingenuity, and certainly Glenée knew that Marie had as much and more of the same.

No surprise, then, that when Marie's daughter, Lisa, announced her engagement, Marie wasted no time enlisting Glenée's assistance with the myriad wedding projects she envisioned. "At first I thought Glenée would have to lead the way, but she said, 'Oh, no, you don't need me, but it would be fun to do it together.' It was so delightful working with her—blending our talents and ideas. That is part of what I will always cherish about Lisa's wedding, the way we shared it with

friends, both the work and the play." Because Marie is passionate about her garden, a seasonless masterpiece of perennials and pergolas, she wanted to feature the summer's success in the fall wedding. Marie and Glenée decided to use pressed flowers as decorative accents on the table place cards.

They collected and pressed as many flowers as they could. Marie remembers, "Phone books were everywhere, oozing with pansies, daisies, rosebuds, fern, dianthus, and scaveola.

"Once the flowers dried, Glenée came over for a long afternoon, and we assembled everything, painting the backs of the flowers with toothpicks of craft glue and then sticking them onto beautiful paper that Glenée had watercolored with numbers, names, and ribbons. All this we did

while gossiping and eating chocolate cake. The best fun there is!"

Then there was the wedding cake topper. Marie couldn't find anything that resembled Kurt and Lisa as a couple, but ingenuity saved the day again. "We improvised with a plain bride and groom. Glenée and I bought lots of tiny pearls, simple narrow lace, thin white ribbon, and a few tiny white fabric flowers and redecorated the arch over the couple's heads and the base. Glenée even painted the groom's hair blond to match Kurt's, and then we hot-glued it all to my tiniest lace doily and pedestal cake plate.

"How could it not be pretty?" Marie exclaims. "By then everything, every single detail, had such an enchanted place in our hearts."

basket sachets

Most women love the idea of a small gift. A little present holds the magic of an intimate thought. A sachet that has the added gift of fragrance is one of my favorites. Make these vintage flower basket sachets from scraps of fabric saved for their loveliness or sentimental meaning. The flowers that decorate the top edge are made from ribbons twisted into blossoms. If you prefer, use purchased ribbon flowers or make them from wool felt to create a bouquet effect.

SO SHALL A FRIENDSHIP FILL EACH HEART
WITH PERFUME SWEET AS ROSES ARE,
THAT EVEN THOUGH WE BE APART,
WE'LL SCENT THE FRAGRANCE FROM AFAR.

— GEORGIA MCCOY —

ENLARGE THE PATTERN on page 152. Fold the fabric in half, right sides together, pin the pattern to it, and cut out two baskets. Stitch along all sides, leaving an opening in the top where indicated. Turn the fabric right side out and fill with the sachet filling. Blind-stitch the top opening closed. If desired, use pearl cotton and a running stitch to create a basketweave pattern on the front of the basket.

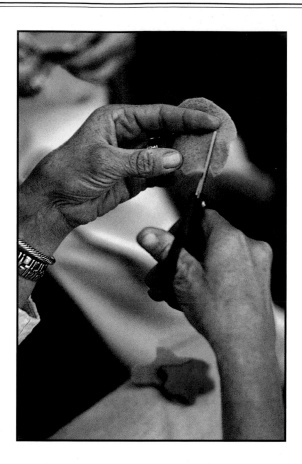

you will need

- TRACING PAPER AND PENCIL
- A SMALL PIECE OF FABRIC, 6" X 12"
- STRAIGHT PINS
- SCISSORS AND WIRE CUTTERS
- NEEDLE AND THREAD
- SACHET FILLING OF YOUR CHOICE, SUCH AS DRIED LAVENDER, ROSEMARY, OR CEDAR
- PEARL COTTON TO MATCH FABRIC AND EMBROIDERY NEEDLE
- RIBBON LENGTHS OR PURCHASED RIBBON FLOWERS OR SCRAPS OF FELT
- SCRAPS OF FELT, CUT INTO SMALL DISKS
- GOLD CORDING WIRE OR RIBBON FOR THE BASKET HANDLE
- 4 GLASS BEADS TO SEW TO BOTTOM EDGE

To make a ribbon flower, take a length of ribbon about 6 inches long. Twist to make a rosebud center and stitch to the center of a 3/4-inch disk of felt. Continue twisting and blind-stitching the twists to the felt disk to make additional petals. Attach the felt and ribbon flower to the top of the basket. Continue to add flowers, as well as leaves made from small ribbons folded as for a bow tie.

Cut the cording for a handle and sew to the basket. Sew beads to the bottom edge if desired.

FRIENDSHIP IS LOVE WITH UNDERSTANDING.

— ANONYMOUS —

potato print box

Potato prints are a quick way to add style and pattern of your own design to just about anything you wish to decorate. They are especially effective for small boxes that have flat, even surfaces to stamp on. Mixing and matching the roughly carved stamp shapes with bright, contrasting colors lead to inventive combinations and a great deal of fun. Make this little jewelry box for a friend and fill it with a cache of funky jewelry from a thrift shop.

ENTHUSIASM IS CONTAGIOUS. BE A CARRIER.

— SUSAN RABIN —

your design with small cuts (1/4 inch deep) to reveal a stamp. Use a foam brush to paint the stamp portion of the potato and test stamp on a paper towel to see the true form of the design. Stamp the box as planned. Add accents, such as the flower center and leaf, with stamps made from scraps of potato. The evenness of the paint will vary and is part of the folk art look, so don't fret if some applications skip a bit. You can go back and dab in paint with a cotton swab or artist's brush wherever you want.

When dry, seal the box outside with two coats of acrylic varnish. Paint the ball feet and glue them at the corners. Allow to dry overnight. In the center of the lid, attach a screw eye. Then attach a hanging charm with needle-nose pliers and wire.

IF THE BOX IS OLD, be sure to clean it thoroughly and prime it with white paint before painting the decorative coat. If it is new, sand the edges lightly and wipe away the dust. Although it is usually a good idea to prime the box first, I did not prime this one because I liked the way that the paint was taken in by the unfinished wood, as if it were a stain. Then simply paint the interior of the box and the outside panels on the sides and top with colors that you like. Allow to dry with a loose nail or some other space holder placed between the lid and the bottom so that the paint does not seal the lid shut.

Then cut a potato in half and draw a design on it that can be roughly carved away with a kitchen knife. Rather than create very complex designs, use simple shapes and combine them for detailed designs. Cut away the potato from

you will need

- A PLAIN WOOD BOX RECYCLED FROM A GARAGE SALE OR PURCHASED NEW FROM A CRAFT STORE
- WHITE PRIMER OR SANDPAPER
- ACRYLIC PAINTS AND SEALER
- FOAM BRUSHES
- POTATO, PENCIL, AND PARING KNIFE
- PAPER TOWELS
- 4 WOODEN BALLS TO ADD FOR FEET (OPTIONAL)
- GLUE
- SCREW EYE AND WIRE
- CHARMS, BEADS, OR AN OLD EARRING
- NEEDLE-NOSE PLIERS

HEARTFELT PILLOW

PAGE

70

MEMO BOARD

PAGE

72

DUMPLING SOUP

PAGE

76

all day

Surely there are lots of reasons to save a whole day for crafting—especially if you are in the company of friends. Some projects that are fairly easy might need more time for different reasons. Papier-mâché, for instance, takes a while to dry, so there is a welcome amount of down time when you can relax and chat with a friend between the stages. Put the teakettle on.

WHEREVER YOU ARE, IT IS YOUR OWN FRIENDS
WHO MAKE YOUR WORLD.

— WILLIAM JAMES —

CACHEPOTS

PAGE

78

PAINTED HANDBAG

PAGE

86

SEWING BOX

PAGE

92

BIRDHOUSE

PAGE 80

POSTCARD HOLDER

PAGE 82

VALENTINE POCKETS

PAGE 88

seat is full of wonderful, secondhand stuff waiting to be transformed by your exhilaration and creative tinkering. By the time you have finished brainstorming, it might be lunchtime. It's a good idea to plan ahead so you can make soup (recipe included),

This is when new ideas will come to mind and plans will take shape for more chances to make and do. Perhaps your project requires a bit of hunting and gathering to find the right materials or inspiration. You could spend a whole day simply scouring tag sales, which is great fun in itself. Before you know it, the back

recharge, and get on with your project. If the day disappears too quickly, make plans to finish later or just give in and keep going. This kind of creative experimenting is so invigorating and strangely thrilling that you will find yourself stretching out a project as much as possible. The best is yet to come.

heartfelt pillow

Tug at those heartstrings by stitching up a little felt pillow for a friend. This small pillow also seems just about right for a ring bearer if you happen to have a friend heading down the aisle. What could be more wonderful than a handmade keepsake contributed by a friend?

CUT OUT A HEART from the square of red felt and use sewing thread to stitch it onto the rectangle backing. With the thread, randomly stitch X's on the rectangle. Sew a button or charm onto the center. Pin the completed rectangle onto the fabric backing and use the pearl cotton and a blanket stitch to attach it. With the pearl cotton, make a long running-stitch maze pattern on the backing that repeats the shape of the heart rectangle. Right sides together, sew the two pillow pieces front and back to each other, leaving an opening. Turn the pillow through the opening and stuff. Stitch closed. Make tassles by cutting the tassle strip into four 2-inch segments. Roll the piece of wool tightly together so that it resembles a stick. Stitch through the roll on one end to hold it shut. Securely wrap the stitched, rolled end with pearl cotton. Use scissors to cut

the opposite end into fringes that end just below the pearl cotton wrap. Take care not to snip the pearl cotton wrap. Sew the rolled end to a corner of the pillow and repeat for the remaining corners and tassles.

you will need

- 3" x 3" SQUARE OF RED WOOL FELT FOR THE HEART
- SEWING THREAD AND NEEDLE
- 3" x 4½" PIECE OF WOOL FELT FOR THE RECTANGLE BACKING THE HEART
- A BUTTON OR CHARM
- 9" x 9½" PIECE OF FABRIC FOR THE PILLOW BACK
- PEARL COTTON AND EMBROIDERY NEEDLE
- 9" x 9½" PIECE OF WOOL FELT OR SOME OTHER FABRIC YOU PREFER FOR THE FRONT
- POLYESTER STUFFING
- 2" x 8" STRIP WOOL FELT FOR TASSLES

memo board

Papier-mâché is fun anytime but is especially good as a snow-storm project. On those days when it snows so much that you can't leave home, a good cure for cabin fever is to make something. Most of these materials will already be on hand, so it's easy to start and fun to finish. Stay in your pajamas or shovel a path to your neighbor's house and sign her up to make something too.

RULES FOR HAPPINESS: SOMETHING TO DO,
SOMEONE TO LOVE, SOMETHING TO HOPE FOR.

— IMMANUEL KANT —

variety of shapes and patterns in the paper. The idea is to make it look as though it is a tile mosaic. Leave spaces between patterns to create a grouted look. Create an eye and beak with this technique. When dry, glue several twigs and silk flowers, leaves, or berries to resemble a nest. Glue a clothespin to each of the three points on the base. Allow to dry undisturbed for several hours.

For the house: Copy and cut out the silhouette on page 154 or make up your own. Consider drawing the shape of a friend's house to use as a pattern. Attach two hangers, as directed above. Cover the silhouette with papier-mâché, as above, then base-paint and decorate with paint colors as shown or as desired. Cover with a coat of acrylic varnish and glue four clothespins to the base.

TO BEGIN, enlarge and transfer the pattern from page 155. To make the bird from cardboard, cut out one bird, one wing, and a base, which is the bird with the attached nest shape beneath. Attach hangers to the back of the base by fishing a wire through each of two evenly spaced holes and twisting shut. These hangers will be covered on the front, but the loops will show on the back. Glue the wing to the bird, and then the bird with wing onto the bird base backing so that it is dimensional. Papier-mâché the entire construction (bird and base), as in the project directions for the *Note Box* on page 40.

When dry, paint the papier-mâché bird and base white. Allow to dry. Paint the base beneath the bird light green. Cut out magazine pictures of blue and white china patterns or fabrics using these to paste and collage the bird with the

you will need

- TRACING PAPER AND PENCIL
- CARDBOARD OR THE SIDE OF A STURDY BOX CARTON
- SCISSORS AND BRUSHES
- 2 LENGTHS OF WIRE
- WHITE GLUE
- FLOUR, WARM WATER, AND WHITE GLUE FOR PAPIER-MÂCHÉ PASTE
- ACRYLIC PAINTS
- MAGAZINES OR CATALOGS TO CUT UP
- TWIGS AND SILK FLOWERS WITH BERRIES AND LEAVES
- 7 CLOTHESPINS
- ACRYLIC VARNISH

:: Activities and Suggestions for a Craft Club ::

STUDY a project from a vintage craft book or a flea market find like the greeting card basket. Figure out a way to make it with modern craft materials. Experiment as a group.

HAVE everyone bring a recycled glass bottle or pot and a sack full of trinkets to the meeting. The hostess supplies premixed adhesive grout and each person decorates her vessel with grout and charms.

SUPPLY the group with small canvas boards, paint, glue, and fabric scraps. After pairing up, each person makes a scrap portrait of her partner.

TRY painting tiles, plates, or pottery with permanent acrylic paints.

CREATE craft kits to take to a children's hospital. Lead an activity there.

PAINT a table and chair set to donate to a women's shelter.

GATHER the materials for an activity like scrapbooking, découpage, or papier-mâché and invite new friends to experiment with the group on an easy project.

INVITE a guest artist or school art teacher from your area to attend your meeting. Ask her to demonstrate her skill and philosophy of creative expression.

HAVE each member bring ten souvenirs from summer vacation and a shadow box. Provide fabrics, decorative papers, glues, and paints so that you can create memory boxes together.

CRAFT CLUB

dumpling soup

This elegant soup recipe is a snap to prepare. Made with Asian-style dumplings, it can be prepared as a vegetarian dish and has a fresh, unusual taste suitable for all seasons. If Asian dumplings are hard to come by in your area, substitute Italian tortellini or ravioli filled with meat or cheese, depending upon your preference.

HEAT THE CHICKEN or vegetable broth in a large pot. Add the minced shallots, garlic, and sesame oil. Simmer 5 minutes. If using tortellini, add those at this point and simmer 6 minutes.

Add the sliced shiitake mushrooms and the sliced scallions. Simmer 2 to 3 more minutes. Add the snow peas, spinach, and cilantro. If using fresh dumplings, add these now. Warm through and serve.

Serves 6.

you will need

- 8 CUPS CHICKEN OR VEGETABLE BROTH
- 2 TABLESPOONS MINCED SHALLOTS
- 1 TABLESPOON MINCED GARLIC
- 1/2 TEASPOON SESAME OIL
- 4 SHIITAKE MUSHROOMS, STEMS REMOVED, SLICED
- 4 SCALLIONS, SLICED DIAGONALLY
- 18 TO 20 VEGETABLE OR MEAT DUMPLINGS, OR 3/4 POUND TORTELLINI OR RAVIOLI
- 1 CUP SNOW PEAS
- 1/2 CUP SHREDDED SPINACH
- 2 TABLESPOONS CHOPPED CILANTRO

cachepots

When I was a teenager, my mother let my friend and me découpage my bedroom dresser, which we happily did, covering it inside and out with magazine cutouts and slogans like "You've come a long way, baby!" It was fun and fabulous, and I was absolutely hooked. Thirty years later découpage is back in style,  more so than ever. Nowadays there is a myriad of products in the marketplace that lend themselves beautifully to the craft. My favorite containers to dress up with découpage these days are made of galvanized tin, like this pair of cachepots. I love the way they look covered in ivory

TO KEEP A LAMP BURNING WE HAVE TO KEEP PUTTING OIL IN IT.

— MOTHER TERESA —

paper, with black type and torn images. Buy the containers inexpensively at a garden shop or import store and sit down with a girlfriend and a stack of catalogs, some paste, and scissors. It won't be long before you are feeling the giddy excitement of school girls.

Decorate each panel with more torn bits of paper, perhaps showing a second style of type or handwriting. Occasionally wrap the paper around a corner to the adjacent side. Finally, add a decorative image or two to each side, such as a catalog painting or botanical.

FOR A SMALLER VERSION of this project, choose a little container—even a coffee can will do—or decorative accessory and use the same technique.

FOR THE HOLIDAYS, mini birdhouses make pretty gifts to use as tree ornaments. Remember to seal the work with a few coats of acrylic varnish.

you will need

- A METAL OR WOOD CONTAINER (PAINTED SILVER) WITH FLAT SIDES
- DECORATIVE PAPER
- SCISSORS
- FOAM BRUSHES
- DÉCOUPAGE MEDIUM
- ACRYLIC VARNISH

CUT OR TEAR paper panels roughly the size of the side panel you wish to cover. Avoid a perfect fit—uncovered metal randomly showing through is part of the overall look. With a foam brush, apply découpage medium to the back of the paper. Apply the paper to the side of the container as planned, smoothing out bubbles and wrinkles. Cover the four sides with background paper in this way. Let dry.

When Donna's son was born, she realized that having a play group would be an important part of his development. She didn't imagine that it would become crucial to her life as well. What began as a casual meeting of babies and moms has evolved into a women's group, a men's group, and a crew of families who even get together for an annual camping trip.

Between Friends: Donna and Friends

Donna explains: "I was desperate to find friends after I moved and had Matthew. It started with four of us—now we are six—getting together and focusing on the babies. I wasn't sure if we would become friends, but it seemed to work. One day when I realized that our husbands were getting together on Saturdays, I thought, 'Wow, we could do other things too!' So we moms began to get together once a month on our own without children or husbands. We would take turns planning the event for the group at home or out somewhere. Six years later we have tried just about everything. Ceramic painting, jewelry making, manicures, book group meetings, wine and cheese tastings, flower arranging, gardening, trunk shows, knitting, découpage, cake decorating, theater outings. We have asked special guests—like someone's mother—to teach us new things, such as how to prepare gefilte fish or how to play mah-jongg. And we have grown very close as women and as families. This is not just about the good times; we have become friends who share everything."

Donna believes that because all of the women were young mothers, their individual differences became a common strength. "We don't share our everyday lives; we live in different towns, our children go to different schools, so the group friendship has broadened our experiences and given each of us greater resources for all kinds of things. We share advice about everything, from getting a child to sleep all the way to starting a business. In fact, I did start a home-based business with another woman from the group, and it's been successful for over three years. There are so many ears, points of view, laughs. We keep each other focused and close to each other, but without the strings that you have with family."

Sometimes she feels as if they are, in fact, a kind of family now. They still spend every New Year's together, and the husbands have their own "men's night out." Donna can drop her children off at a "play group" house and know that everyone is seamlessly comfortable, happy, and at ease. "Now that the kids are older, we have less of a need for a play group and more time to fulfill our own pursuits. Some of the women are closer than others and see each other more often, but it is still great fun for all of us to be together once a month. I cherish and rely on these friends; I feel we are all accepting of each other's personalities. We have truly special friendships that I envision lasting through many years and many milestones."

postcard holder

Postcards are lovely things to collect and send. I have a globetrotting girlfriend who has such exquisite taste and handwriting that the cards

we receive from her become collectible art. I made this little postcard kit for her to keep in her backpack. There is a pocket for the cards, another for addresses or stamps, and the whole thing folds up neatly. The chimney has a buttonhole that serves as a tab closure for all or as a hanger if she should choose to hang it on the wall.

HOME IS WHERE ONE STARTS FROM.
— T. S. ELIOT —

Make this for a friend heading off into the wild blue yonder—as Elaine did. We were very excited to receive a card heralding her successful climb to the top of Africa's Mount Kilimanjaro.

STEP ONE: Although this project has several steps, it is not as difficult as it appears. The house is pieced using the foundation method, in which you actually sew the fabric pieces to a backing paper along drawn pattern lines. Afterward, you remove the paper and have a perfectly pieced block!

Enlarge and transfer the pattern on page 153 onto a piece of vellum paper. Cut four windowpanes pieced from two different fabrics, each 1 1/2 inches square. Using a 1/4-inch seam, sew two contrasting panes together. Press the seam toward the darker fabric. Repeat for the second pair. Place the two pairs right sides together, aligning the center seam. Sew the pairs together, making sure the windowpane fabrics alternate.

Pin the window unit (face up) to the right side of the paper, matching the window crossbars with the corresponding lines on the paper patterns. Cut a piece for the center top section

of the house, the size of the finished piece plus about 1/2 inch extra on each side. Pin the house section face down on top of the window section, aligning the raw edges at the top edge of the window unit. Turn the paper over so you can see the pattern drawing face up with the fabric beneath.

Set the stitch gauge of your sewing machine to a short stitch (approximately 18 stitches per inch), but not too short or the paper will tear

you will need

- COTTON FABRICS IN 8 COORDINATING SMALL PRINTS AND COLORS
- VELLUM PAPER AND BLACK PEN
- STRAIGHTEDGE
- SCISSORS AND STRAIGHT PINS
- SEWING MACHINE
- IRON
- 3 BUTTONS

too soon. Sew along the pattern line, stitching through both the paper and the fabric. Remove the pins and trim seam to 1/4 inch. Open the piece you have just added and press it flat.

Rough-cut the remaining center house section and a door, remembering to add seam allowances. Repeat this "pin, stitch, trim, press" process with the addition of each section. Add the center middle section and then the door, continuing to pin, stitch, trim, and press. Add the house side right and then side left. Trim the finished block to the pattern outline and remove the paper, carefully tearing it away along the stitching lines, which will have perforated it nicely. Do not press again.

STEP TWO: Cut a piece of fabric the same size as the house block. With right sides together, using a 1/4-inch seam, sew the pieces together along the top edge. Open, fold back, and press the seam.

Cut four 6-inch squares of different coordinating fabrics, one for the roof and three for the pockets. To make the roof, fold one 6-inch square in half, wrong sides together, pin, and press. On the side opposite the fold, mark 1 1/4 inches from the corner on each edge. Cut this part away diagonally on each side to create a roof pitch. Set aside.

With the first square right side down, pin it to the bottom of the lined and pieced house. Stitch through house and lining; open and press. Pin the second square to the bottom of the first and stitch, open, and press. Repeat for the third square. Press and check to be sure the strip is straight.

To make the pockets, which are made by self pleating, fold the second square 4 inches up onto the first square, leaving 1 1/2 inches of the second square to fold back for a contrasting pocket top. (Square three remains unfolded.) Pin at the fold and press.

Cut a strip of backing fabric, 6 by 28 inches. Right sides together, stitch the strip to the bottom of the third square. Fold up 4 inches to make the last pocket, then bring the backing strip right side up and fold back down to the bottom edge. Pin at the bottom and press. Baste along the bottom edge of the pocket.

STEP THREE: With right sides together, fold the remaining length of backing strip back onto the house. Turn over and check for straightness. Add the folded, angled roof square, which should be placed and pinned just above house finished edge. Pin along both sides, top to bottom, at regular intervals. Stitch up each side and along the roof sides. Leave open along the rooftop. Trim, turn, and press.

STEP FOUR: To make a chimney and tab closure, cut a strip of roof fabric, 1 1/2 by 4 inches. Fold in half, right sides together, and sew up the sides; turn and press. Make a buttonhole in the center. Insert the unfinished edge of the tab in the middle of the roof opening and fold down the roof seam allowance. Baste closed, then top-stitch close to the edge around all the outside edges, securing the chimney in place.

Top-stitch along the house bottom to make an inside pocket accessible between the roof and the house. Place a postcard inside the bottom pocket and fold the strip in thirds. Add a button where the buttonhole meets the back. Sew a small button on the door and at the window if desired.

Fill the house with a few postcards stamped and preaddressed to you.

painted handbag

While you are scavenging at the church sale, look in the ladies' accessories department for old-fashioned pocketbooks and handbags like the ones Grandma carted around. These are often the best canvases for pop art paint jobs. Clean the vinyl with a little soap and water, then give it a splashy makeover with the spunky style and bright colors fit for a favorite friend.

you will need

- A HANDBAG COVERED IN PAINTABLE VINYL, LEATHERETTE, OR FIBERBOARD
- HOUSEHOLD CLEANER AND PAPER TOWELS
- ACRYLIC PAINTS IN SEVERAL COLORS
- FOAM AND ARTIST'S BRUSHES
- STENCILS, STAMPS, OR HAND-DRAWN DESIGNS
- ACRYLIC SEALER

TO BEGIN, clean the bag with an all-purpose household cleaner, paying special attention to grime that might be on the handle or hinges. Be sure to wipe the cleaning product off completely. Paint the various panels in a variety of colors and allow to dry. Avoid painting any

metal hinges or latches. Using a 1/2- to 1-inch-wide artist's brush and a contrasting color, add stripes to a few sections. Using a thinner brush, add swirls, X's, flowers, dots, wiggles, leaves, and other motifs wherever you like.

Change colors frequently, staying in the same palette of brights or pastels, and repaint any area that you are dissatisfied with. Sometimes the addition of a new design motif will make another one look better. When you are finished, paint your friend's initials somewhere and then seal with acrylic sealer.

valentine pockets

My friend Norah stopped over one day and caught me in the middle of this papier-mâché project. Within moments we had a heart-shaped pocket built for her  too and spent a good part of the afternoon playing around with ideas and designs. Although it was indeed Valentine's Day, the sweet little pocket seems appropriate for all times of the year. Fill it with flowers, presents, or homemade cookies and hang it as a May basket, in a guest room, or just about anywhere at all.

SMILES ARE THE SOUL'S KISSES.

— MINNA THOMAS ANTRIM —

Make the papier-mâché paste by mixing the warm water, flour, and white glue. Dip strips of newspaper in the paste and then slide them between your fingers to remove most of the paste. Paste the strips onto the cardboard as if they were tape, covering all the outside surfaces in different directions, wrapping over to the heart inside about 1 inch. Do not overbuild any particular area and avoid the balled newspaper form.

you will need

- PLAIN PAPER AND PENCIL
- LIGHTWEIGHT CARDBOARD, SUCH AS SHIRT BOARD OR POSTER-BOARD
- SCISSORS
- HOLE PUNCH OR AWL
- MASKING TAPE
- NEWSPAPER AND NEWSPAPER STRIPS, 1" X 6" OR 8"
- 1 CUP WARM WATER
- ½ CUP FLOUR
- 1 TABLESPOON WHITE GLUE
- TISSUE PAPER, FABRIC SCRAPS, OR PAINTS
- GLUE
- RIBBON

CUT OUT THE HEART-SHAPED template (page 157) to use for tracing. Trace and cut one heart from cardboard. Cut a second one the same size. Use the second heart as is or cut it in half for an open pocket. Use a hole punch or an awl to pierce two holes in the rear heart for hangers. Attach the two hearts together at the sides with masking tape. Make a ball of newspaper and firmly stuff the inside of the heart to make it puff out like a pocket.

LITTLE DEEDS OF KINDNESS, LITTLE WORDS OF LOVE,
HELP TO MAKE EARTH HAPPY, LIKE THE HEAVEN ABOVE.

— JULIA FLETCHER CARNEY —

Allow to dry thoroughly with the newspaper ball inside. You can place the heart pocket in a 200°F oven for an hour to speed the drying time.

After drying it in the oven or air-drying it on the table, remove the ball and check to see that the pocket holds its open shape. If not, put the ball back in and add another layer of papier-mâché strips. Repeat the drying process. Remove ball when dry and stable. Reopen the holes in the back if necessary.

Use the template to cut paper or fabric coverings, adding 1/2 inch extra around the edges. Cover the pocket with these pieces, using glue and your fingers to apply them. Wrap the excess material to the back so that it covers the outside edge. Cut a piece for the back of the rear heart that is slightly smaller than the template and glue it in place to cover the wrapped edges. Hang with a ribbon cut to the desired size.

FLOWERS ALWAYS MAKE PEOPLE BETTER, HAPPIER, AND MORE HELPFUL;
THEY ARE SUNSHINE, FOOD, AND MEDICINE TO THE SOUL.

— LUTHER BURBANK —

sewing box

Make a sewing box and pin cushion pretty enough that your friend can leave it out on the table. This bare box from the craft store needed only a little paint and a few bits of fabric and trim to become a lovely home accessory. It can also double as a jewelry keeper if the top is used for decorative pins rather than straight ones.

TO BEGIN, prime and then paint the box sides in a decorative pattern. I used a square cut sponge that I alternately dipped into different paint colors to make a checkered pattern. Then I used the sponge again and overpainted some parts with gold. Add a layer of acrylic sealer or varnish. When dry, cover the top of the box with a few squares of quilt batting to build up a pin cushion. Use a staple gun to anchor these near the top edge of the lid so that you can staple the fabric cover to the lower edge. Cut a coordinating fabric piece large enough to wrap down onto the sides. Staple into place neatly, making clean miters at the corners. Cover the staples by gluing trim into place. Let dry. Make

or purchase a decorative flower to tack at the center of the top or perhaps use a decorative piece of costume jewelry. Inside, finish the box with decorative paper, fabric, or paint.

you will need

- A WOOD CRAFTER'S BOX OR CONTAINER SUITABLE FOR AN UPHOLSTERED TOP
- FOAM BRUSHES
- PRIMER
- ACRYLIC PAINTS AND SEALER OR VARNISH
- SCISSORS
- QUILT BATTING
- FABRIC TO COVER THE TOP
- STAPLE GUN
- DECORATIVE RIBBONS OR TRIMS
- GLUE
- RIBBON FLOWER OR ONE MADE FROM FELT
- DECORATIVE PAPER FOR INSIDE (OPTIONAL)

JOURNAL

PAGE

96

TOPSY-TURVY DOLL

PAGE

100

WALL CLOCK

PAGE

104

over the weekend

I have been fortunate to steal an occasional weekend away with the girls. When I come home tired and bleary-eyed, my family asks why I am not refreshed and ready to jump back into the routine. Even though it is a vacation of sorts, I'm usually worn out from staying up all night talking and listening, laughing and doing silly things that college roommates might.

THERE WAS A DEFINITE PROCESS BY WHICH ONE MADE PEOPLE
INTO FRIENDS, AND IT INVOLVED TALKING TO THEM
AND LISTENING TO THEM FOR HOURS AT A TIME.

— REBECCA WEST —

CARD BASKET

PAGE

106

TEA COZY

PAGE

110

FELT HEART ORNAMENT

PAGE

120

LEAF COLLAGE

PAGE 116

TEA COZY

PAGE 110

PUPPY PILLOW

PAGE 118

on the calendar before you even go home. Maybe you have a women's group already formed or a circle of girlfriends that will take to the idea of an experimental weekend getaway. All you have to do is plan it and they will come. Rent a cottage at

I never want to miss a thing, and there can be lots to do, depending upon everyone's interests. This is a terrific way to make lifelong friends out of new ones or to take care of old friendships scattered across the miles. A single weekend of crafts and fun can easily mushroom into an annual tradition etched

the beach or in the country or go to an arts camp where everyone learns a new craft or turn your house into a getaway retreat—just for a weekend. Get your projects together, plan a menu, take some field trips, and the good times will roll right along— faster than most of us can keep up.

Take advantage of a friend's know-how and learn how to needlepoint. On a getaway retreat, appoint her to take charge of a simple project that everyone can explore and finish up while the weekend fun percolates. Needlepoint canvas comes in a width that will easily accommodate several personal samplers. A bouquet of colored threads and a simple design will make it quite appealing. Build a fire, put on afternoon tea, and get to it. Warn the girls in advance, though, to bring their reading glasses—this is simple but fine work.

LITTLE HOUSE YOU ARE SO SMALL,
JUST BIG ENOUGH FOR LOVE, THAT'S ALL.

— ANONYMOUS —

home

you will need

- TRACING PAPER AND PENCIL
- PERMANENT MARKER AND MASKING TAPE
- 4" x 6" PIECE OF NEEDLEPOINT CANVAS: SIZE 14
- PEARL COTTON IN RED, LIGHT GREEN, DARK GREEN, GOLD, BROWN
- TAPESTRY NEEDLE
- SCISSORS
- CRAFT KNIFE AND STRAIGHTEDGE
- A PIECE OF CARD STOCK OR HANDMADE PAPER, 3½" x 5"
- GLUE STICK AND WHITE GLUE
- AN OLD LETTER OR OTHER DECORATIVE PAPER
- PAPER EDGERS
- A JOURNAL, 6" x 9"
- RUBBER STAMP ALPHABET

TRANSFER THE PATTERN from page 155. Use a black marker to trace it onto the center of the canvas, leaving a border around all edges. Use the masking tape to edge the canvas and keep it from raveling.

Begin with the gold thread and work the front door with a diagonal needlepoint tent stitch. Working from right to left (top right to bottom left), bring the needle up through the top right corner square of the door, leaving a 1-inch tail of thread on the back. Insert the needle diagonally to the left and below, making a half cross stitch. Bring the needle back up in the square directly above and repeat the stitch diagonally to the left. While you are stitching, hold the thread tail with your left hand and stitch over

it on the back to secure it in place. Repeat this stitch for the row below but reverse directions from left to right, bottom to top. When you are ready to change colors, weave the thread through a few stitches on the back and clip.

Work the red house but leave the window unstitched so that the white canvas remains. It looks like a little wood mullion, and I prefer to leave it unworked, but you may stitch it if that's your preference. Work the roof and chimney in brown, the fence and tree trunk in brown also. Use the dark green for the tree and grassy hill. Then work the background in light green. When finished, press and straighten the work with a press cloth and steam iron.

Using a craft knife and straightedge, cut out a mat from the cardstock that perfectly matches the dimensions of the finished needlework. Leave extra space (3/4 inch at top and sides, 1 1/2 inches at bottom) below the work to attach a stamped title. Be sure that none of the white canvas shows around the edges.

Use white glue to glue the mat to the needlework. Allow to dry, then glue the matted needlework to the letter or decorative paper background. Cut with decorative paper edgers to fit the front of your journal and leave a border around the mat.

On a scrap of letter, rubber-stamp your initials, a name, or a title. Trim, edge, and glue to the mat with the glue stick. Glue the letter-backed needlework plaque to the front of the journal, cover with a sheet of aluminum foil, and weight with several books until dry.

topsy-turvy doll

Remember the dolls we had as children that flipped upside down to reveal a second doll hidden under the skirt? I always thought my doll connected by a common skirt was my best friend and me. Make this mixy-matchy doll pair to represent you and your best friend, living separate lives but "joined at the hip." Actually, they really are.

AFFECTION IS THE BROADEST BASIS OF GOOD IN LIFE.
— GEORGE ELIOT —

with a disappearing pen and stitch in place using small stitches or small French knots. Lightly color the cheeks with colored pencil.

Baste the shirt front to the body front, right side facing up. (You can skip this step by using fusible bonding, or create a shirt afterward, as I did with one doll.) Repeat for the back and then for the second doll front and back. Right sides together, pin and stitch doll A front to doll A back through all four layers of shirt and doll. Repeat for doll B. Remove the basting for the shirt, turn, and stuff each doll separately.

Stitch the two dolls securely to each other at the waist, faces up. This seam will be permanently hidden by the skirt after it is applied.

Fold the skirt fabric in half, right sides together, and stitch 1/4 inch from edge. Machine- or hand-gather at each end of the skirt tube, folding the raw edge down 1/4 inch to the wrong side as you sew. Turn right side out, slip over the dolls, and gather one waist to fit doll A, stitching by hand and securing 1/2 inch below the armpits all around the waist. Repeat for the waist of doll B at the remaining gathered edge.

The skirt will form a self hem when you pull the skirt down over one doll to cover the underneath doll. Turn upside down to reveal the second doll.

BEGIN BY TRANSFERRING the patterns from page 156 to tracing paper. Cut out and set aside. Pin the shirt pattern to the shirt fabrics and cut out so you have a front and back for each doll shirt. Fold down the four shirt neck edges and blind stitch. Repeat for the sleeve edges at the hands or leave unfinished. Set aside.

Pin and cut out the body pieces for both dolls. Lightly mark the placement of the eyes and mouth

LITTLE TASKS MAKE LARGE RETURN.

— BAYARD TAYLOR —

you will need

- TRACING PAPER AND PENCIL
- SCISSORS AND STRAIGHT PINS
- 10" x 12" PIECE OF DOLL BODY
  FABRIC FOR DOLL A,
  SUCH AS LINEN OR MUSLIN
- 10" x 12" PIECE OF DOLL BODY
  FABRIC FOR DOLL B,
  SUCH AS MUSLIN OR LINEN
- 10" x 10" PIECE OF FABRIC
  FOR DOLL A SHIRT
- 10" x 10" PIECE OF FABRIC
  FOR DOLL B SHIRT
- 20" x 20" PIECE OF FABRIC FOR
  DOLL SKIRT THAT COORDINATES
  WITH BOTH SHIRT FABRIC CHOICES
- NEEDLE AND THREAD IN
  ASSORTED COLORS
- RED OR PINK COLORED PENCIL
  AND DISAPPEARING PEN
- FUSIBLE WEBBING (OPTIONAL)
- POLYESTER STUFFING
- QUICK PULL WOOL DOLL HAIR
  PACKS IN TWO COLORS
  (CRAFT STORE DOLL SECTION) OR
  RAFFIA IF YOU PREFER
- ASSORTED LENGTHS OF RIBBON
  AND TRIM FOR DECORATION
- BEADS, BUTTONS, AND WIRE
  FOR DECORATION

For hair, cut a shank of doll hair or raffia about 6 inches long. In the middle of the length, stitch it securely to the top of the doll's head. Repeat with a second length and stitch to the back of the head. Fluff the hair by pulling apart the strands into individual waves and allow these to fill out a head of hair. Decorate with a ribbon to tie up into an attractive style. Make a necklace out of beads or buttons that can be sewn to the doll front. A bracelet can be fashioned from brass wire wrapped around the wrist.

HOLD A TRUE FRIEND WITH BOTH YOUR HANDS.

— PROVERB —

wall clock

Ihave a friend who works too hard and needs an occasional "wake-up" call to get her out of the office. If you have a friend like that, make a clock for her that is pleasant to look at, one that will remind her that the world awaits her return. With the availability of quick clock parts at craft stores, homemade clocks are amazingly simple to create. You can make them out of almost anything—a plate, a book, a board. I used a piece of foam core and covered it in my usual découpage collage. All the images are themed to the natural world—a place without computers, telephones, or fax machines.

CUT AN INTERESTING shape from the foam core or cardboard that is big enough so that the clock hands can circulate freely. Identify the center spot for the clock, measuring to be sure it is centered side to side. With an awl, push a hole through that center mark and enlarge with a pencil to allow the clock stem to fit. Set aside the clock parts and decorate the rest of the clock by découpaging with paper and cutouts. Wrap all paper edges to the back and cut out a back cover piece slightly smaller than the clock shape. Glue in place to cover the wrapped edge. Add ribbon trim if desired, and charms also, using wire and pliers. Use the pencil to reestablish the clock stem hole. Cut and glue twigs to the top and bottom for a decorative frame. Assemble the clock according to package directions. The clock mechanism has a built-in hanger.

you will need

- A BATTERY-OPERATED CLOCK MECHANISM WITH HANDS
- FOAM CORE OR CARDBOARD THAT ACCOMMODATES THE LENGTH OF THE CLOCK STEM
- MEASURING TAPE, AWL, AND PENCIL
- DECORATIVE PAPERS, RIBBONS, WIRE, TWIGS, AND CHARMS
- FOAM BRUSHES
- DÉCOUPAGE MEDIUM, SUCH AS MOD PODGE
- CRAFT GLUE, SCISSORS, NEEDLE-NOSE PLIERS, FLOWER CUTTERS

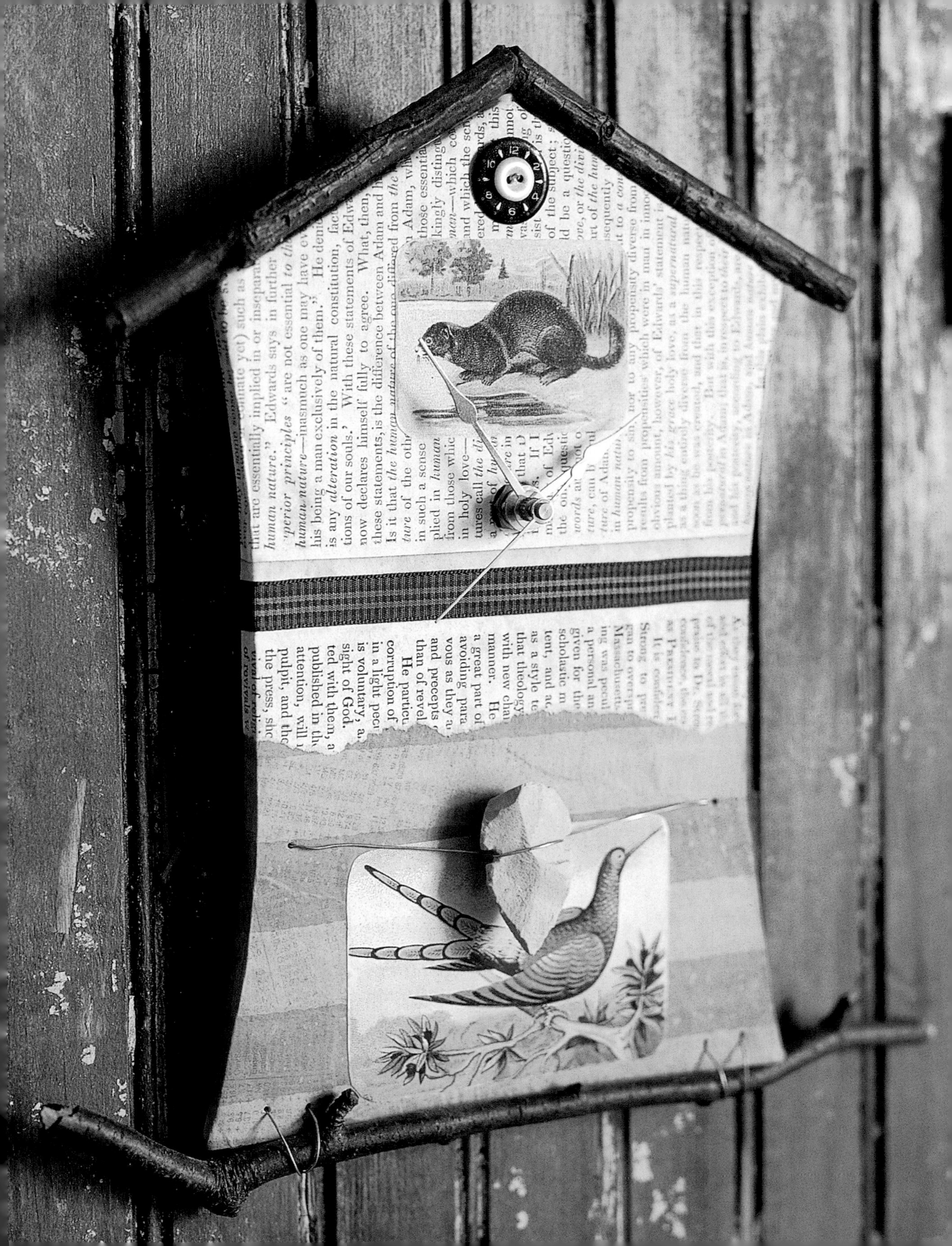

card basket

Many exceptional pieces of artwork and illustration are available as greeting cards or postcards. If you find it hard to part with some of these pretty samples or perhaps keep them because a dear friend wrote you a note inside, this project makes excellent use of that saving instinct. Use the cards themselves or make color copies of them. Be sure to copy some of the script inside too. Seeing the familiar handwriting of a friend has a powerful ability to evoke fond memories.

YESTERDAY IS NEVER OVER. YESTERDAY ENDURES FOREVER.

— JEHANNE D'ORLIAC —

of raffia on a tapestry needle, lace each panel to the one beside it, ending with a bow or knot at the top. When you have joined the eight panels into a ring, use the raffia to whip-stitch the top, first in one direction and then in the other.

Place the finished basket round on a piece of cardboard. Trace the interior bottom shape. Mark the panel joints on this circle and also mark a matching notch to one particular panel to ensure later placement fit. Remove the basket bottom and add an extra 3/4 inch all around the tracing. Cut out.

BEGIN BY enlarging the pattern on page 156 for the side panel. Transfer this to poster board and cut out a template. Use a hole punch to create holes as indicated on the pattern. Trace the template onto seven more pieces of poster board. Cut these out with a craft knife and punch holes in each. Trace the template onto a piece of white paper and cut out the interior shape, leaving a window in the paper the size of the template. Use this window to identify the best part of each greeting card image or photocopy that you will be cutting according to the template. Trace the inside lines of the template window and cut out the greeting card or copy. Punch holes to match the template.

Use spray adhesive to spray the backs of the cards or copies and attach to the fronts and backs of the eight panels. With a 24-inch length

At each joint mark, cut out a V and fold the tab to the inside. Drop the basket bottom into the basket as planned, allowing the folded tabs to come up on the inside. Mark the placement of holes from corresponding panels on each bottom tab. Remove and punch holes in the tabs to match. Apply a decorative paper to the basket bottom if desired. Use raffia to lace the bottom to the basket all around.

:: Activities and Suggestions for a Knitting Club ::

TAKE a common pattern and knit scarves or blankets to donate to a charity. (Many organizations and ideas are listed at www.knitting.about.com.)

BE the mystery guests at a friend's baby shower, where you help each guest start a knitted square. When the guest finishes her square, she sends it back to your group. Assemble the various handmade squares for a finished baby blanket to give the new mother.

LEARN to knit a new technique, such as knitted lace.

ORGANIZE member-led workshops at which a member teaches a new craft to the group. It might be yarn embroidery, weaving, or some other yarn-related craft.

PLAN a field trip to an exhibition or gallery show of textile arts. Many museums have textile archives that they rotate through special shows.

KNIT baby blankets for a children's hospital or women's shelter.

COLLECT yarn remnants to exchange with group members or donate them to a preschool art room. Ask to be invited back for a gallery show of the children's finished art projects.

USE the *Book Bag* pattern (page 44) to make knitting bags that store patterns and projects in the works.

KNITTING CLUB

tea cozy

A friend and I discovered the model for this tea cozy in a church thrift shop. When I turned around and saw her with an embroidered knit hat on her head, we had a good laugh about such a strange hat with holes for ears. Of course, after looking at it closely, we recognized its true identity—a tea cozy. To make a pattern for the thrift shop cozy, I used the hat model and knitted a few different versions until I found my favorite: sized to fit my coffeepot, ribbed and decorated with charms and flowers. It knits up so quickly that you could make it in an afternoon and then make one for a friend too. The decorative trims transform the traditional knitted cozy into an exceptional gift.

THANK GOD FOR TEA! WHAT WOULD THE WORLD
DO WITHOUT TEA? HOW DID IT EXIST?

— SYDNEY SMITH —

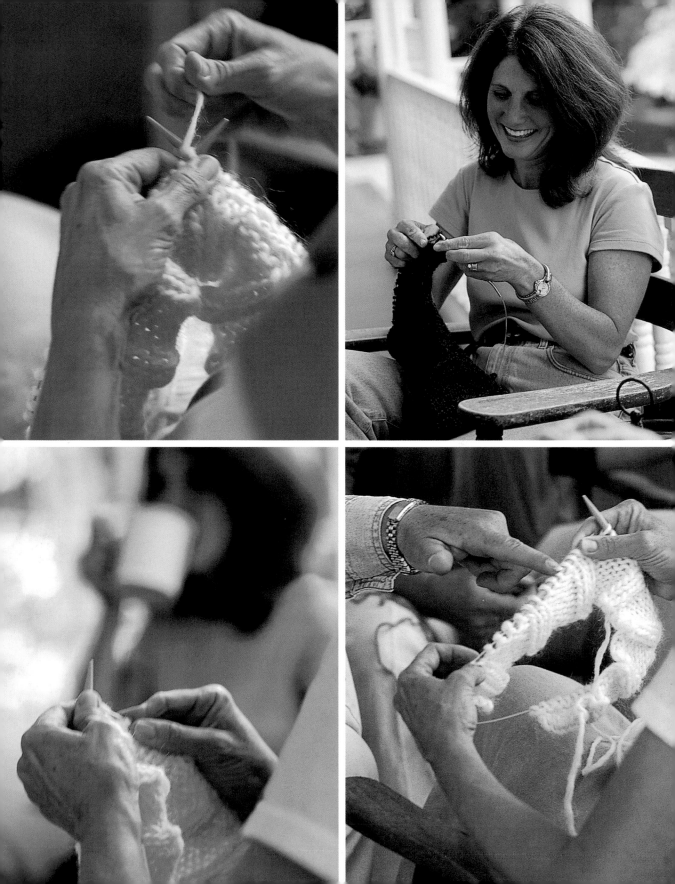

— ribbed version —

CAST ON 46 stitches. Knit 4, purl 2 first row. Purl 4, knit 2 back. Continue in this pattern until you have knitted approximately 2 inches or until you have reached a measurement that fits your teapot's spout bottom. With front of work facing you, K4P2 for 22 stitches and then knit together stitch 23 and 24. Turn work and knit 2 together, then continue in pattern for 3 inches on the right side only. Break yarn and work left side to match without decreasing stitches. Join sides by working across, then increasing 1 in last stitch on right and first stitch on left. Continue in ribbed pattern for 4 inches. With front of work facing you, decrease by

K1K2 together across so that you have 31 stitches remaining. P3K1 back. Continue ribbed pattern for 4 rows. K2 together all stitches so that 16 stitches remain. K1P1 for 3 rows. Next row knit and increase every stitch. Purl back, cast off. Place cozy on teapot with spout in knitted opening. Pin and mark where handle fits on other side. Using yarn and a tapestry needle, stitch above and below handle. With another length of yarn, gather at cozy neck, draw up, and tie off. Place on teapot to adjust for fit if needed.

With one side facing you, use the tapestry needle to work the ribbon up the middle purl channel at 1 1/2-inch intervals. Work second decorative trim over ribbon, if desired. Use sewing thread and a needle to stitch into place, snipping ribbons at top and bottom. Tie a small bow from remaining wide ribbon and stitch at top of ribbon stem. Add flower and charm as desired. Repeat for other side.

— checkered version —

PICTURED ON PAGE 114

CAST ON 48 stitches and K3P3 for 4 rows, then reverse to P3K3 for 4 rows to achieve a checkered pattern. Follow above directions except Ktog stitch 24/25 for opening. When work measures 5 3/4" high, begin decreasing K1, K2 tog, P1, P2 tog for one row. Knit 3 rows K2P2, then 2 rows P2K2. For neck, K2 tog all stitches. Purl back. Knit in stockinette 4 rows. Increase every knit stitch next row, purl back, then knit one row, purl one row, and cast off.

Use a tapestry needle and 2 colors of crewel wool to add daisies with the daisy stitch to alternating squares.

you will need

- 1 SKEIN (100 GRAMS) REYNOLDS LOPI WOOL YARN IN IVORY (COLOR 51)
- KNITTING NEEDLES, SIZE 10.5 OR SIZE TO ACHIEVE GAUGE OF 3.25 STITCHES TO AN INCH

RIBBED VERSION:
- TAPESTRY NEEDLE
- 48" IVORY EYELET RIBBON 3/4" TO 1" WIDE
- 20" DECORATIVE RIBBON TRIM IN GREEN (OPTIONAL)
- SEWING THREAD AND NEEDLE
- 2 SMALL IVORY SILK FLOWERS WITH LEAVES
- 2 BRASS CHARMS OR BUTTONS

CHECKERED VERSION:
- TAPESTRY NEEDLE
- CREWEL OR KNITTING WOOL IN 2 COLORS

J anet knitted a sweater in college and that was it. For thirty years she never had time for knitting again. She raised a family, pursued a career, changed communities, and finally allowed herself to look up and see what the rest of the world was doing. Janet saw that many women had managed to develop friendships that she now envied. They were having fun together doing things like knitting.

Between Friends: Janet and Friends

Even after living in her new town for five years, Janet felt unconnected until she met a woman who knitted beautifully and enthusiastically. Janet knew this was her much-awaited chance for friendship, creative expression, and blissful relaxation. A few coaching sessions with her friend and she was hooked. Since then, Janet has knitted everything under the sun, learned to spin, founded a spinner's group, joined a knitting guild (of which she has been the president), won competitions, and loosened the crippling arthritis in her hands. In a word, she is passionate about knitting.

But the centerpiece of this life transformation has been the far-reaching development of a personal community. "There are three or four of us who started out as knitters with a common interest, but there is so much more to our relationship now. I have three

sons and a husband who see me doing this day and night, but they don't truly understand how much it means. These women get it—they know that this is part of my soul because they feel the same way. They understand *completely*."

That intuitive understanding can't help but spill over into the rest of their lives. "We support each other through everything, through the tough times, any kind of crisis. And we have used our support and our knitting knowledge to help others, too. We knit for charity, for people all over the world who simply need comfort. It's a way to give something very personal, something tangible that holds its meaning. By now I am knitting endlessly anyway. I can knit through meetings at work, on the soccer sidelines, at the doctor's office. Why not? It actually keeps my mind more

focused." Janet and her friends knit together and apart. They have held workshops with guest speakers and sat in each other's living rooms over coffee as well. The Internet has given them wide access to experts in the craft, who rapidly become friends too. When making a pattern or struggling with a stitch problem, the knitters log on to a knitting listserv, post a question, and receive several answers within a day. "This group of like-minded women has been my anchor. It really is so hard as an adult to make connections. Everyone is increasingly busier, off at a job, tending children. It is awesome to me to feel connected to women now, and also to those down through the centuries who depended on needlework to support and clothe their families. I'm always amazed at how much my life was changed by just two sticks and some string."

leaf collage

Take a walk with a friend on a beautiful day and collect some of the colorful fall leaves offered freely along the way. Once home, carefully store them inside a heavy book for pressing. It's a good idea to tag the book and tie it shut so you don't forget that there are leaves or flowers drying inside. Later you will find them undisturbed and ready for a project. Use the different shapes to build a picture like this little fairy cottage in the woods. Consider building it to resemble your friend's house and garden.

THE EASIEST WAY to start is to select a department store picture frame that you can take apart. Then create the collage to fit the frame interior. Remove the interior liner sheet and use it as a pattern to cut a backing paper to fit. Arrange the leaves into a pleasing collage on the backing paper, allowing the different colors and shapes to dictate the placement. Remember to leave empty space around the edge of the collage so that the blank paper acts as a mat border as well. To make a house, choose a leaf that is not too brittle and trim it with sharp scissors only where needed so it resembles a house profile. Add smaller leaves for roof lines, door, and windows, trimming those as needed. Pressed flowers can become shrubbery or pathways. Small leaves look like trees when they are applied with their stems. Once you have a general layout, lift each leaf and dab the back with dots of glue applied with a toothpick, then place it back into the collage. Allow to dry undisturbed. Pencil a quote beneath all or simply add your signature and date. Reassemble after cleaning the glass.

you will need

- FRAME WITH GLASS
- ARTIST'S PAPER TO USE AS BACKING PAPER
- SCISSORS
- PRESSED LEAVES IN A VARIETY OF SHAPES AND COLORS
- PRESSED FLOWERS FROM THE GARDEN OR THE CRAFT STORE
- CRAFT GLUE AND TOOTHPICKS

puppy pillow

Seven mornings a week, I meet a group of friends in a field where we talk, walk, and sip coffee while our dogs run around and play. Kind of like play group, it is delightful. We are all a bit silly about dogs and their place in our lives, so it's no wonder that this pillow design came to be. Though it's not really a great likeness of Jake, my golden retriever, it is a good use of some wool scraps in the basket. My favorite part is the fringed plaid scarf that appears as the grassy field. I hope to make portrait pillows for the whole doggy gang—maybe for the holidays. The basic shape can be altered easily to get a rough look-alike of any pet. Make this easy pillow for a friend who cherishes her pooch. She will absolutely love it.

THERE IS NO POSSESSION MORE VALUABLE
THAN A GOOD AND FAITHFUL FRIEND.
— SOCRATES —

118

—felt heart ornament—

Use some of the same wool scraps to make this little ornamental heart. Cut two heart shapes, one a bit smaller than the first and handsew them together with a decorative stitch like this feather stitch. Use the sewing thread to sew a paper image into place and then attach a small button and raffia bow. A small piece of ribbon or trim makes a hanger.

READ ABOUT HOME-FELTING on page 151. Enlarge the pattern on page 157. Adapt the shape by redrawing to portray your pet. Lengthen or shorten the tail and legs or reshape the ears and muzzle. Make a copy of the new design and cut out for a pattern.

Choose a wool color that fits the dog. Cut out the dog shape and pin to the background. With matching sewing thread, blanket-stitch the shape in place. Add a collar with a contrasting bit of wool and satin-stitch the eyes and nose with crewel yarn. Place a strip of wool beneath the dog's feet and stitch in place. If using a fringed scarf, leave the fringe unsewn so that it resembles real grass. Using matching crewel wool, blanket-stitch the orange rectangular background onto the plaid pillow front.

Place the pillow backing on the finished pillow front, right sides together, and sew all around, leaving an opening to turn and stuff. After doing so, blind-stitch the opening closed.

you will need

- TRACING PAPER, PENCIL, AND SCISSORS
- WOOL FELT IN THE COLORS SHOWN OR THOSE YOU PREFER:
  - 8" x 11" ORANGE FOR DOG BACKGROUND
  - 7" x 9" YELLOW-GOLD FOR DOG
  - 2" x 7" GREEN WOOL PLAID FOR GRASS
  - 12" x 15" WOOL PLAID FOR THE PILLOW FRONT
  - 12" x 15" BACKING FABRIC FOR THE PILLOW BACK
- STRAIGHT PINS, SEWING THREAD, AND NEEDLE
- WOOL CREWEL YARN IN MATCHING COLORS FOR DOG'S EYES AND NOSE AND FOR STITCHING BACK-GROUND ONTO PILLOW BACKING
- POLYESTER STUFFING

GARDEN THROW

PAGE

124

CRAFT CABINET

PAGE

128

HOOKED RUG

PAGE

132

as long as it takes

The process of celebrating our friendships is one that carries us away in new directions. Some of our crafts and hobbies are the same way. Like dear friends, they grow with time to fill special needs in our creative lives, fostering self-discovery and fulfillment. Getting together in a group, in a pair, or simply working alone with a dear friend in mind, women can stretch the boundaries of traditional craft with fresh, original interpretations.

OUR AFFECTIONS ARE OUR LIFE.
WE LIVE BY THEM; THEY SUPPLY OUR WARMTH.

— WILLIAM ELLERY CHANNING —

MEMORY BOX

PAGE

136

FRIENDSHIP QUILT

PAGE

140

SCRAPBOOK

PAGE

146

your own vision with your choices in materials or modified designs.

Many of the projects in this chapter are, indeed, labors of love. They take

We delight in the making of beautiful, artistic things because it lets us share who we are—our quirkiness, talent, joy, and affection.

These projects that require so much time should especially reflect your particular talents and ideas. Use the patterns as inspiration for uniquely expressive versions. Try adapting a project to

WEEKEND PRESERVED

PAGE 139

more time, more imagination, more hands, more soul. That is the best part, I think. Made as a gift, the finished piece amounts to far more than the combination of simple materials, design, and workmanship. In such a grand, personal effort, the message is unmistakable: "I cherish you, dear friend, so very much."

garden throw

Having a friend come for an overnight stay is a good excuse to make the house sparkle. She is going to notice things that the usual gang might not, and she will delight in every little effort to make her feel special. Even if you don't have a permanent guest suite, you can pamper her with a temporary princess retreat dressed to welcome her arrival. Poofy pillows, fresh flowers, and brand-new linens and towels are a good start. For a comfy chair tucked into the corner, make this pretty garden throw out of appliquéd wool felt. Set a stack of dreamy magazines nearby, and she may never leave.

THE BEAUTY OF THE HOUSE IS ORDER,
THE BLESSING OF THE HOUSE IS CONTENTMENT;
THE GLORY OF THE HOUSE IS HOSPITALITY.

— HOUSE BLESSING —

the black background using a hem stitch and reversing the same stitch to achieve a cross-stitch effect. Use this same stitch at the strip ends to join the panels.

Enlarge and transfer the flower patterns on page 158 to stiff paper. Cut out eighteen flowers, centers, and small centers in a variety of colors, mixing and matching to achieve the desired color effect when stacked as flowers. Stitch all the centers to the flowers with a simple hem stitch and set aside. Cut out fourteen 3-inch disks and coordinating centers. Stitch the centers in place on the larger disks. Cut twelve 2-inch disks for the two short ends. On the flattened blanket, arrange and pin the flowers and colored disks along the edge, placing at even intervals and aligning the flower center at the edge of the green strip for placement. Stitch in place. Dry clean only.

READ ABOUT FELTING on page 151. You can use a purchased blanket throw or make your own with a length of black wool from the fabric store. Choose wool that is soft to the touch or consider making the project out of fleece. It will be softer and easy to work with because the edges will not require finishing. That is also the beauty of wool felt, which I prefer for its lasting quality.

Cut the green felt into assorted lengths, all 5 1/2 inches wide. Spread the blanket on a flat surface and pin the green strips along the edge, leaving 1/2 inch of black blanket along all the sides. Overlap the strips 1/2 inch where they meet. Aim for a pleasing transition between green tones and keep the strips varied for color interest and a folk art look. Stitch the strips to

you will need

- 1 BLACK WOOL BLANKET, 45" x 78", OR 2 1/2 YARDS OF BLACK WOOL OR FLEECE, 54" WIDE
- 3/4 YARD EACH OF 3 DIFFERENT GREEN WOOL FELTS
- ASSORTED COLORS OF WOOL FELT IN JEWEL TONES FOR FLOWERS
- BLACK SEWING THREAD
- SCISSORS, NEEDLE, AND STRAIGHT PINS
- CARD STOCK FOR TRANSFERRING FLOWER PATTERNS
- PENCIL OR PEN

:: Activities and Suggestions for a Quilting Club ::

ORGANIZE a group show at a local coffeehouse so that you can exhibit your work as a group.

MAKE at least one quilt to donate to a charity raffle every year. Consider working with the children at a school, where your members can teach them the craft and help them design the quilt for a school fund-raiser.

EACH member chooses a simple color scheme, like red and yellow. Every other member makes a 5-inch block in that color-way for that person's quilt. Once a month, one collection of colored squares is assembled and quilted for that member.

GO to a museum shop, where each member chooses a postcard of a painting in the museum. Each member makes a miniature challenge quilt that uses only the colors shown in that painting.

FOR a birthday celebration, each member comes to the meeting with four pieces of quilt fabric bundled in a pretty way. Fill a basket and present the collection to the birthday girl.

AT a church sale, buy old cotton dresses that can be washed and cut up for vintage quilts. Use the fabric to mend old quilts or to make new ones with vintage patterns.

LEARN a new technique, such as photo transferring on fabric, computer design, or miniature quilting.

QUILTING CLUB

craft cabinet

A day of "tag-sailing" is much more fun if you have friends to shop with and a mission to fill. Pool your pennies and big ideas while hunting down a perfect piece of furniture to make over as a group house-warming gift or donation to a charity (think: local preschool art room, women's shelter, or senior center). This secondhand utility cabinet was a good choice for a group project because it had lots of drawers to experiment with using small patterns and different styles. Decide on a common paint palette, then let each crafter have a drawer and a potato to carve. Swap uniquely designed stamps and discovered paint secrets while working together—laughing all the way.

USE IT UP, WEAR IT OUT, MAKE IT DO OR DO WITHOUT.

— NEW ENGLAND PROVERB —

using an uncarved potato, as shown on the top here; other stamps were added over the rough stamped circle. Consider using the small scraps shed from the carving, too. Use the foam brush to add details like stripes, and be sure to paint the knobs as well. If possible, use the rubber stamp alphabet to stamp a label for each drawer, such as Ribbons, Charms, Buttons.

To finish, seal with two or three coats of acrylic sealer. Cut decorative papers, such as these copies of an old sewing magazine, to fit the inside walls and bottoms of the drawers. Glue into place. If time allows, use the potato stamps to make your own liner paper, notecards, gift wrap, or anything else that strikes your fancy. Unfortunately, potato stamps do not last much more than a day.

TO BEGIN Clean and base-paint the piece in the color of your choice. This cabinet was painted with three similar greens, striated over each other to create a dimensional look. Then use potatoes carved with small shapes and designs that can be combined to make bigger designs. Draw a design on a halved potato and use a paring knife or craft knife to cut away 1/4-inch-deep chunks of the potato, leaving the raised design as a stamp. Patterns for these are shown on page 158, but you will enjoy making up your own. Use a foam brush to paint the potato stamp the color you wish to stamp. Stamp on newsprint first to see what the true pattern is and then start on the piece.

As each stamped color dries, begin to layer the stamps on the drawers, sides, and top. Different color combinations with the same stamps will give an entirely unique impression overall. Try

you will need

- A PIECE OF FURNITURE WITH FLAT SURFACES SUITABLE FOR STAMPING
- BASE PAINT COLOR, SUCH AS THIS GREEN
- POTATOES AND KITCHEN PARING KNIVES OR CRAFT KNIVES
- FOAM BRUSHES
- ACRYLIC PAINTS IN GREENS, LIGHT BLUES, YELLOW, ORANGE, AND BLACK
- NEWSPRINT
- RUBBER STAMP ALPHABET
- ACRYLIC SEALER
- DECORATIVE PAPER AND GLUE
- GLUE STICK OR SPRAY ADHESIVE

hooked rug

Rug hooking is a craft that women have pursued for pleasure and creative expression for hundreds of years. Like needlepoint and embroidery, hooked imagery worked on a length of woven backing is richly textured, sturdy, and individual in style. Prized for its "folk-artness," a hooked rug is an extraordinary personal project or gift. Rug hookers are passionately devoted to their craft, and if you like this process, you will make many, many rugs in the years ahead. More important, you will find

PASSION, THAT THING OF BEAUTY, THAT FLOWERING WITHOUT ROOTS,
HAS TO BE BORN, LIVE AND DIE WITHOUT REASON.

— GEORGETTE LEBLANC —

friendly faces and eager companions in any rug group, guild, or class you locate. Delighted to share techniques and materials, members often swap patterns or extra bits of wool. I returned home one day to find a bundle of wool on my doorstep, compliments of a friend who knew I could use what she found. It included my favorite color of red, and every time I look at the rugs in which I have used that color, I thank Emmy for her thoughtful gesture that day.

BEGIN BY ENLARGING and transferring the pattern from page 159 onto the backing, keeping the pattern drawing straight to the weave of the backing. Finish the raw edges of the backing with two rows of machine stitching all around to prevent fraying, then set up the design in your frame with the figure in the center to be worked first.

Cut the collected wool into strips cut to 3/8-inch wide and 12 inches long. Organize them in a basket according to color. Using a rug hook, hold the strip of wool beneath the frame with your left hand and poke the hook through the top of the backing with your right hand. Catch the strip onto the barb of the hook beneath and draw it up through the fabric to create a 3/8-inch-high loop. Release and repeat this motion right beside the first loop.

Continue until you have a "caterpillar" of loops in a row and reach the end of the strip of wool or the space you wish to fill. Do not hook through every hole—the aim is to create a rug

HAPPINESS WALKS ON BUSY FEET.

— KITTIE TURMELL —

pile, but you should not be able to see fabric backing from the top. The beginning and ending tail ends of the strip must remain on the top of the work to lock the strip in place. Clip the ends to match the height of the other loops.

You can go in any direction, but do not cross over other strips or twist the wool strip as you work. When you look on the back of the work, it should be smooth; on top, the backing should not show through. Work the design according to the pattern and photograph.

When you are finished, block from the back with a steam iron and damp towel. Sew rug tape around the edges to conceal the folded hem of unfinished backing. To hang, attach a muslin sleeve across the top on the back. Insert a dowel with an extra inch at each end.

you will need

FOR A RUG OR MAT MEASURING
22" x 14.5":
- PERMANENT MARKER
- RUG BURLAP OR MONK'S CLOTH,
  28" x 21", FOR THE BACKING
- SEWING MACHINE
- RUG HOOK AND FRAME
- RUG TAPE, 2½ YARDS, AND NEEDLE
  AND THREAD TO FINISH
- WASHED AND FELTED WOOL CUT
  INTO ⅜" STRIPS IN THE FOLLOWING
  COLORS AND SIZES (BASED ON
  60" YARD GOODS):
    — MAUVE FOR EDGE AND
    BACKGROUND, ½ YARD
    — BROWN-BLACK TWEED FOR
    BACKGROUND, ⅛ YARD
    — PINK-BROWN TWEED FOR
    ANIMAL, ⅛ YARD
    — PINK FOR FLOWERS AND
    BORDER, 12" SQUARE OR
    SUITABLE SCRAP
    — CRANBERRY RED FOR BORDER
    AND EYE, 12" SQUARE OR
    SUITABLE SCRAP
    — GREEN-BLUE FOR STEMS AND
    BORDER, 12" SQUARE OR SCRAP
    — OLIVE GREEN FOR BORDER
    AND EYE, 12" SQUARE OR SCRAP
    — INDIGO BLUE FOR BORDER,
    12" SQUARE OR SCRAP
    — COFFEE BROWN FOR ANIMAL
    OUTLINE, 12" SQUARE OR SCRAP
- STEAM IRON AND DAMP TOWEL
- MUSLIN FOR A HANGING SLEEVE
  (OPTIONAL)
- DOWEL, 2" LONGER THAN
  TOP OF RUG (OPTIONAL)

memory box

There are many things that will not be compressed into a scrapbook, even though the trinkets are tiny. These diminutive treasures sometimes hold greater meaning for friends who have shared a past or an adventure from which they were collected. A diary key, school pin, worry pebble, rubber-band ball, souvenir matchbox, or seashell. These objects become visual links to memories. Gather the lot onto a tray and collage them into a shadow box, one that ties each to the other in a flowing montage. Using a common color scheme, such as ivory and black, keeps it easy on the eye.

THERE'S NOTHING WORTH THE WEAR OF WINNING,
BUT LAUGHTER AND THE LOVE OF FRIENDS.

— HILLAIRE BELLOC —

YOU CAN USE an old box or a cigar box with the lid removed. Take the box to a hardware store or glass cutter and have glass cut to fit. Brass corners can be used to attach the glass to the box when it is finished. Be sure an older box has a clean inside, free of dust and grime that will keep any glue from adhering properly.

Begin by attaching a hanger to the box back if it does not already have one. Then start arranging the objects loosely in the box with an eye for composition. Do the objects themselves have a similar feature or create a pattern of size and shape? A few seashells might be more interesting placed beside an acorn or lined up on the edge of a feather. Look for unusual extras to add to the collage, such as a vintage ruler, game piece, fabric square, or playing card. Use these to add interest as dimension and background.

Once you have a pleasing arrangement, sketch the general placement of the collage on a piece of paper and remove the objects. Attach background decorative papers with craft glue, then lay in the collage as planned, using small amounts of glue.

When complete, make a legend, a kind of directory of the important objects, using the collage as a guide. Paste the legend onto the back of the box. Be sure to clean the glass first before sealing the box closed.

you will need

- A SHADOW BOX WITH A GLASS FRONT
- BRASS CORNERS, IF NEEDED
- COLLECTED OBJECTS
- PAPER AND PENCIL
- DECORATIVE PAPERS
- CRAFT GLUE

MEMORY IS TO LOVE WHAT THE SAUCER IS TO THE CUP.

— ELIZABETH BOWEN —

Weekend Preserved

After a guest stay at a friend's weekend house, make a little diorama to hold a trinket souvenir or a fallen nest. It could be a collectible, a lonesome salt shaker, an ornament. As a thank-you present, this 3-inch clay figurine and souvenir spoon make a bigger statement inside a big glass jar. As for a terrarium, fill it with dried moss, a silk flower sprig, a pretty card, and a pebble or shell. Then place the figurine or what-have-you in the scene and top with a gingham square and a raffia bow. Ta-da!

friendship quilt

So much of the art of quilting is about friendship and sharing. Beginning with the age-old quilting bee, women have long enjoyed each other's company and expertise along the edges of a quilt frame. Growing by leaps and bounds in popularity, this traditional craft is well loved and avidly pursued today by women who delight in the artistry and power of the needle. These days it is not unusual to see a quilting project emerge from a briefcase on the subway or to find more than one quilting guild in a neighborhood.

THE TINIEST GARDEN IS OFTEN THE LOVELIEST.

— VITA SACKVILLE WEST —

There are as many variations on the friendship quilt as there are personal styles of expression. You might include shared fabrics, signatures on blank blocks, or appliqué flowers contributed by each quilter. A small quilt like this one is quite manageable as a gift project, especially for those of us who might not have the time to make a full-sized quilt as a present. On the receiving end, it is perfect for wall or table display, a daily reminder of dear friends, like flowers ever blossoming on the vine.

somewhat creative. The finished pieced back should measure 14 by 22 inches.

There are three different constructions used to appliqué the vine and flowers. The vine is made by cutting a 1 1/4-inch strip of green fabric 30 inches long on the bias (two shorter sections will also work). Fold wrong sides together, stitch down the length 1/4 inch from the edge, trim to 1/8 inch, and press so that the seam is centered in the back. (A bias bar helps for this step.) Place according

AFTER WASHING and pressing all the cotton fabrics, build a background by creating three strip panels of randomly sized and colored blocks according to the pattern on page 160. The center strip panel is a bridge that joins the right and left strips. If you prefer, enlarge the pattern on a copier and assemble the top using the foundation described in the *Postcard Holder* project (page 82). The appliqué is worked on the top of this, so the construction can be

you will need

- ASSORTED COTTON FABRICS IN BLUE, LAVENDER, AND GREEN
- 1/2 YARD FOR THE BACKING AND BINDING
- QUILTING THREAD AND SEWING THREAD
- NEEDLE, SCISSORS, DISAPPEARING QUILT PEN
- FREEZER PAPER FOR APPLIQUÉS
- VELLUM FOR FOUNDATION PIECING
- QUILT BATTING

to the pattern and appliqué this to the backing with small blind stitching.

The flat flower and leaves are built on freezer paper. Cut out the pattern shape from freezer paper and pin to the fabric with the shiny side of the paper against the wrong side of the fabric. Cut out the fabric with a 1/4-inch seam allowance. Press. The freezer paper creates a temporary bond. With basting thread, fold and baste the raw edge of the fabric against the paper, sewing right through the paper but close to the edge. Refer to the pattern for placement. Using matching thread and a small blind stitch along the fold, stitch the flower or leaf to the pieced backing with the paper in place, but leave 1/2 inch unsewn.

Remove the basting thread and use the needle to coax the paper away from the stitched flower inside, bringing the paper out through the 1/2-inch opening. Finish the blind stitching. If you prefer, you can snip an opening in the pieced backing under the appliqué and pull the paper out through that slit. The batting and backing will conceal the slit later. Do not press the appliqués again.

The yo-yo flowers are built by cutting out a disk 3 inches in diameter. Fold the edge over 1/8 inch and stitch around the disk close to the fold, then draw up the stitches to make a smaller puff. Press the puff flat with the gathers in the center. Sew through the yo-yo gathered center to the back. Mark five petal spots with the disappearing pen around the flower with the gathers facing you. Bring the thread from the back around to the front and insert the needle back inside the center. When you draw this thread tightly over the marked spot, it will create an indented side of a petal. Repeat for the other petals and tie off in a knot on the back. Other flower centers are made by creating smaller yo-yo's without petals. Tack into place where desired or according to the pattern. It is nice if several people have contributed fabrics and flowers to decorate the vine.

Layer the top to the batting and center over the backing wrong side up, with excess all around to use as self-binding if you choose that method. Baste into place. Quilt by hand without a hoop, using matching quilting thread and your own pattern. This one has little leaves and vines quilted in the available spaces and otherwise follows the shape of the appliqués. I use the backing as self-binding, but many quilters prefer to bind with separate strips. Whatever method you choose, finish by hand.

Like many women who sew, Lisa is enchanted by fabric and collects remnants wherever she goes. The closets in her cottage are brimming with small-print calicos waiting to be stitched into quilts, vintage bark cloth destined for curtains or pillows, stripes and dots bundled for baby dresses. Although she sews frequently, Lisa often relied upon her friend, Kathi, to stir her imagination with fresh project ideas.

Between Friends: Lisa and Kathi

When Kathi and Lisa moved to opposite ends of the country, Lisa missed her creative partner and found herself adrift in an ocean of cotton. As it turned out, Kathi felt the same way, so they stitched up a plan to get their projects underway again.

Lisa explains: "We would tell each other all about our sewing projects and started sending swatches to each other with the idea that seeing that bit of fabric was a good way to share our new lives. That was such fun that it turned into a friendship quilt idea. We picked a pattern with smallish pieces like the herringbone, and now every time each of us makes something, like a baby dress or a curtain, we cut two extra pieces of fabric from the scraps to fit the template. We keep one and send the other in a letter with the story of its meaning. It's become a great way to blend two lives with something tangible. I can't say that the quilt is made, but it's certainly developing nicely. Sometimes when I get a letter with a new fabric piece in it, I feel like I'm there. I can almost see the dress she made for her daughter. Soon enough, I'll get out the rest of the pieces and just play around with the whole bunch, wondering what Kathi is doing with her fabric. Of course, then I have to call her and hear about all the details."

Kathi and Lisa are such close friends that they know instinctively what the other would like, even though it's not necessarily what they would choose for themselves. The challenge is to blend the two preferences, which is why it's a good idea to use a small pattern piece. Since they both have daughters, Kathi and Lisa have considered scaling back the big idea into a pair of friendship doll's quilts. That way the children can enjoy them also, and they will be small enough to hang on the wall later.

Lisa recently gave birth to a son and is remodeling her home. "I don't think I'm going to have much time left for sewing—other than curtains, anyway—but I sure look forward to those little fabric letters. It's the next best thing to having Kathi sitting right here next to me!"

scrapbook

Scrapbooking has become a national pastime, it seems. Kitchen tables everywhere have become design stations where women are clearing out junk drawers and photo boxes, organizing bits of ephemera into categories, and filling scrapbooks with personal legends and clever artistry. Clear a table, invite the girls over, and celebrate the birthday of a friend with a handmade scrapbook created especially for her. Although there is no shortage of beautiful paper, consider creating your own by color-copying an old textile. This scrapbook cover features a copy of an antique shawl, a sentimental and unique keepsake in itself.

I WEAR THE KEY OF MEMORY,
AND CAN OPEN EVERY DOOR IN THE HOUSE OF MY LIFE.
— AMELIA E. BARR —

add the initial, which you have backed with a small piece of decorative paper or card stock. Glue buttons in place and a hanging charm or key near the top.

Fill the pages with the multitude of memories you claim together, designing each with the same artistic flair. Save a page for the new snapshots of the presentation itself and the party to follow. You can get together again at a later date to put those into the book.

MEASURE THE EXACT dimensions of the album cover and cut a template from scrap paper to fit, leaving 1/16 inch of cover showing around the edges. Check for a perfect fit and cut the decorative paper to fit exactly. With paper-bonding craft glue and a foam brush, paint the back of the decorative paper and apply carefully to the cover, using a soft, clean dish towel to press out the air bubbles and wrinkles. Allow to dry. Repeat for the copied photo.

Add a length of ribbon with the craft glue so that it bisects the cover vertically where desired, overlapping the photo. When the ribbon is dry,

you will need

- A BLANK SCRAPBOOK OR PHOTO ALBUM
- SCRAP PAPER
- DECORATIVE PAPER OR COLOR-COPIED TEXTILE
- CRAFT GLUE ESPECIALLY FORMATTED FOR BONDING PAPER
- FOAM BRUSHES
- SOFT DISH TOWEL
- COPIES OF AN OLD PHOTO OF THE GIRLS
- 18" DECORATIVE RIBBON
- AN INITIAL FROM A COPYRIGHT-FREE CLIP FILE
- CARD STOCK BACKING
- 3 VINTAGE MOTHER-OF-PEARL BUTTONS
- CHARM OR A DIARY KEY
- SMALL RIBBON SCRAP

WE MUST ALWAYS HAVE OLD MEMORIES AND YOUNG HOPES.

— ARSENE HOUSSAYE —

sources

note:

Local bookstores and libraries have excellent how-to guides available for most craft techniques. Most materials are available at local craft, art, fabric, or hardware stores.

A. C. Moore
888-686-8965
www.acmoore.com
Arts and crafts supplies

Calico Corners
800-213-6366
www.calicocorners.com
Decorator fabrics and trims

Dorr Woolen Mills
603-863-1195
www.dorrwoolen.com
Rug-hooking supplies and wool

Harry M. Fraser Co.
336-573-9830
www.fraserrugs.com
Rug-hooking supplies, patterns, strip cutters, kits, books, catalog for mail order

JoAnn Fabrics and Crafts
818-739-4120
www.joann.com
Supplies and materials, books, and classes

Keepsake Quilting
800-865-9458
www.keepsake quilting.com
Quilting supplies, kits, fabrics, mail order catalog

Michaels
800-MICHAELS
www.michaels.com
Materials and supplies, books, and classes

Plaid Enterprises
800-842-4197
for customer service and technical support.
www.plaidonline.com
Acrylic paints, Mod Podge, découpage medium, and accessories

Wal-Mart
800-WALMART
www.walmart.com
Craft supplies, books, and materials

Walnut Hollow
800-950-5101
www.walnuthollow.com
Wood products and accessories, clock movements and accessories

Waverly Fabrics
800-423-5881
www.waverly.com
Decorator fabrics

online sources

www.about.com
Extensive online resource for most hobbies, including knitting, quilting, needlepoint, embroidery, rug hooking, jewelry, beading, and more

www.noqers.org
Quilting source online

www.rughookers network.com
General information and sources

www.rughooking online.com
Expert advice and information

www.woolworks.org
Knitting advice and information

STITCH GUIDE

blanket stitch   cross stitch   daisy stitch   running stitch

glossary

Acrylic paints and sealer Water-based paints that are widely available, easy to use, and inexpensive.

Appliqué A fabric shape that is sewn onto the top of another fabric. Raw edges are turned under when the shape is stitched into place using a blind stitch.

Batting The lofted, puffy filling inside a quilt. Available at all fabric stores in a variety of dimensions.

Découpage medium Adhesive formulated for paper découpage. Alternatives include white glue, Mod Podge, artist's gesso, gel medium, or wallpaper paste.

Drying time Varies according to the amount of moisture in the product, the air, and the application.

Embroidery floss The most common embroidery thread available. Generally made from six strands, it can be separated for a variety of thicknesses.

Felting A process that binds wool together after exposure to heat, agitation, and moisture. Achieved by placing wool fabric or knitted material in a washing machine full of hot water and running through a wash cycle. Further felting occurs in the dryer, if desired.

Pearl cotton A twisted, corded floss available in a variety of gauges numbered 3, 5, 8, and 12.

Quilting stitch A running stitch used to bind the layers of a quilt together.

Right sides together The finished or design side of two pieces of fabric placed facing each other so that after seaming, the seam will be hidden on the back or inside.

Rug burlap and monk's cloth Foundation material for hooked rug making. Available through catalogs and rug supply shops. Differs from craft burlap in fiber strength and regular weave.

Rug hook A hook that resembles a crochet hook set into a wooden handle. Used to hook wool strips through a foundation material.

Seam allowance Additional fabric needed when sewing two pieces together. Generally, 3/8 inch is the width to allow.

Selvage Factory-woven edge on the lengthwise sides of fabric.

Transfer pen Used to transfer a design from paper to fabric, following manufacturer's instructions. Ink disappears over a short time.

Transferring large patterns After enlarging a pattern on the copying machine, cover the pattern with tulle netting. Use a marker to trace the pattern onto the tulle. Then place the tulle onto the rug backing. Trace again so that ink traces through tulle onto fabric.

Wool yarn Also called Persian yarn or crewel wool, it comes in small bundles for needlepoint and embroidery work.

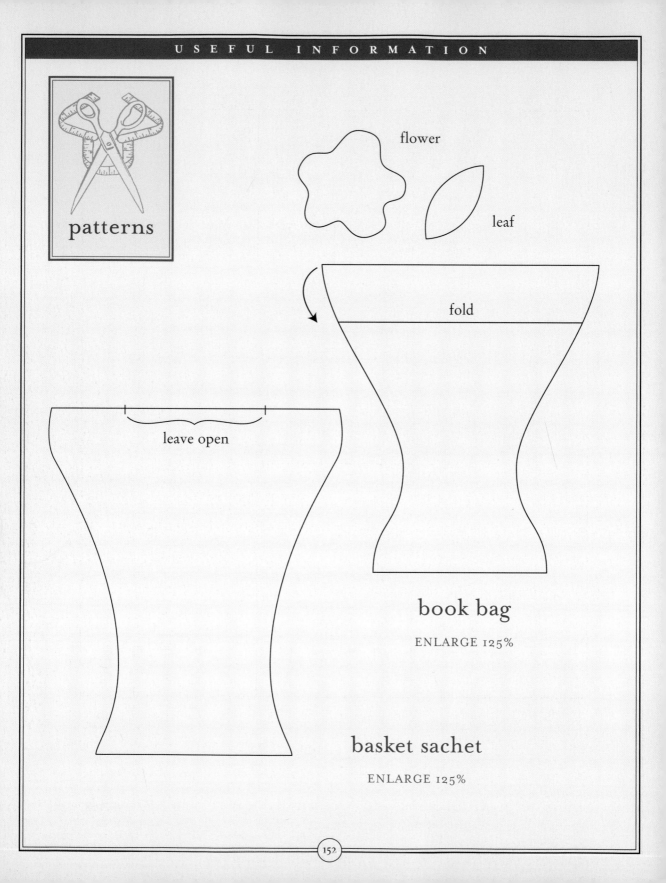

patterns

flower

leaf

fold

book bag

ENLARGE 125%

leave open

basket sachet

ENLARGE 125%

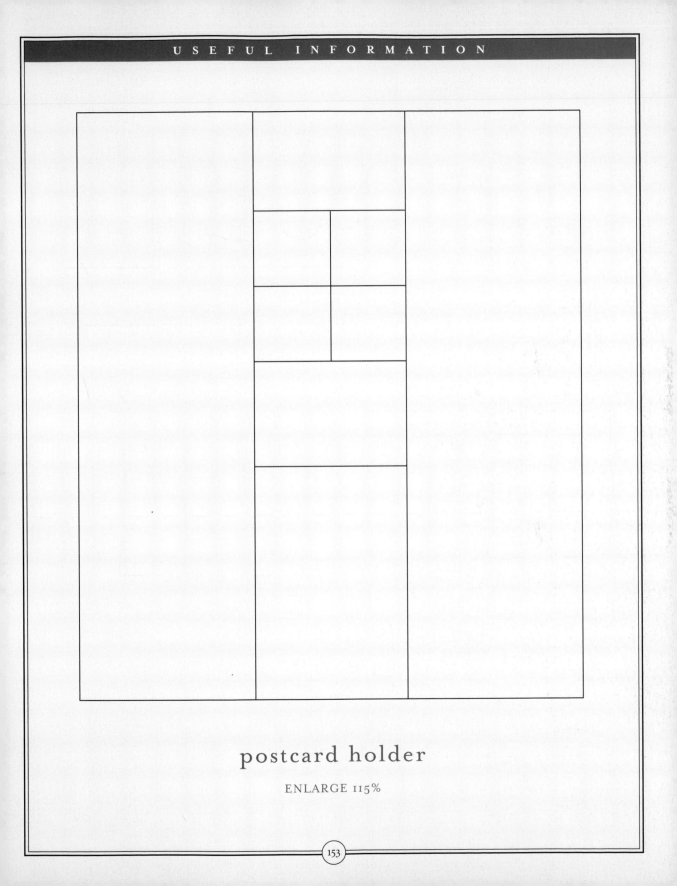

postcard holder

ENLARGE 115%

memo board

ENLARGE 255%

scissors keeper

ENLARGE 175%

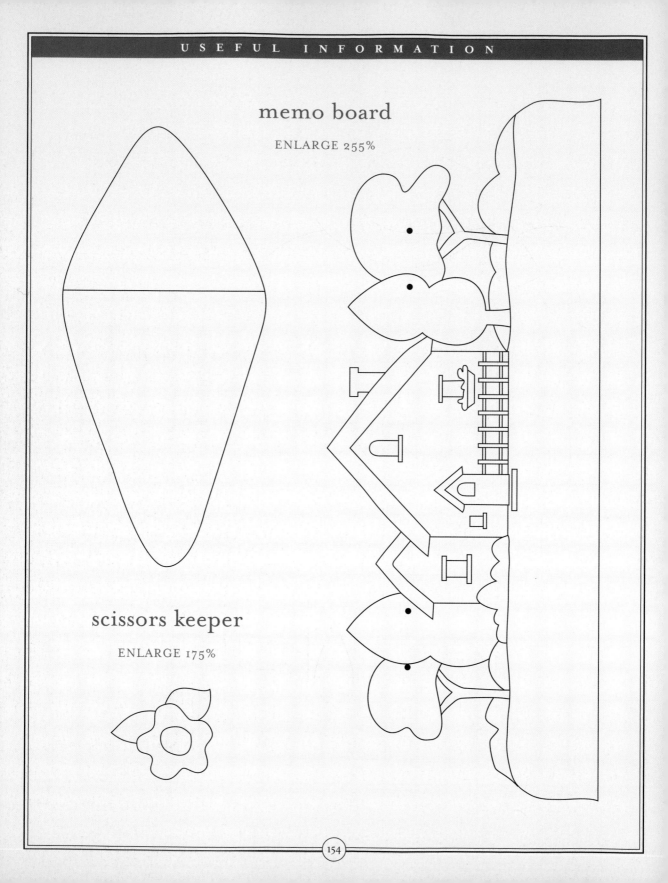

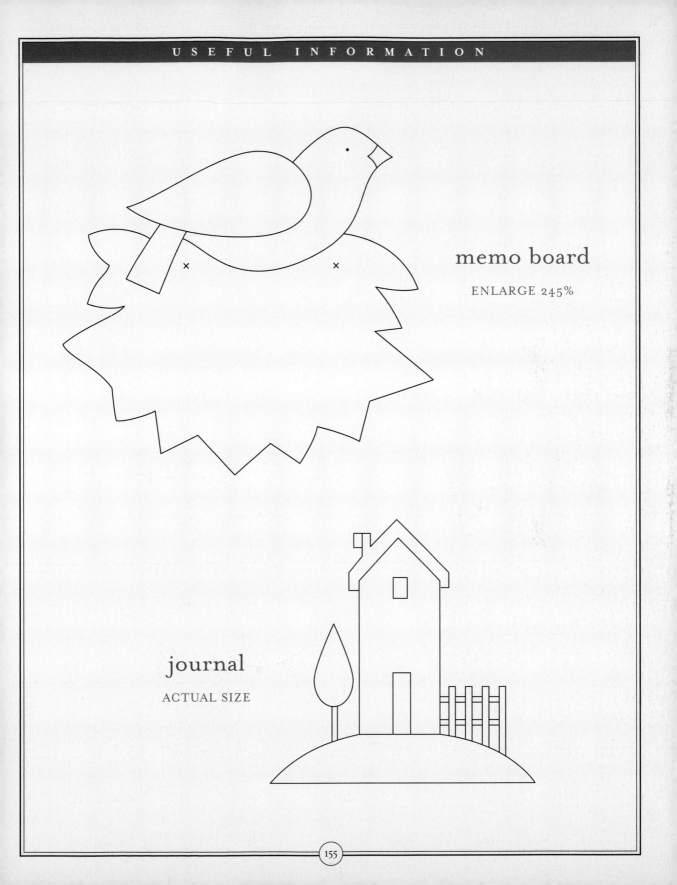

memo board

ENLARGE 245%

journal

ACTUAL SIZE

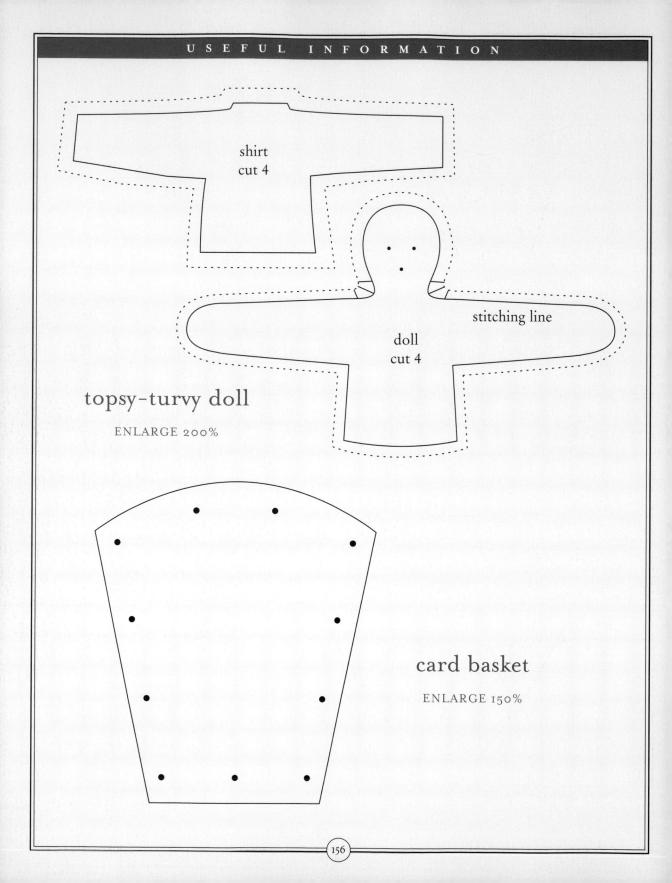

shirt
cut 4

doll
cut 4

stitching line

topsy-turvy doll

ENLARGE 200%

card basket

ENLARGE 150%

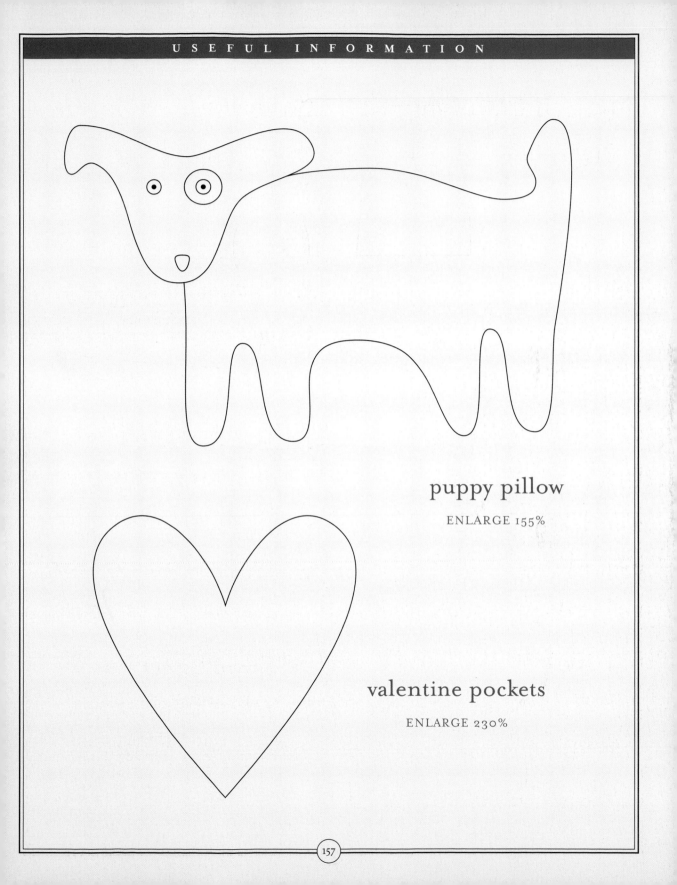

puppy pillow

ENLARGE 155%

valentine pockets

ENLARGE 230%

garden throw

ENLARGE 210%

craft cabinet

ACTUAL SIZE

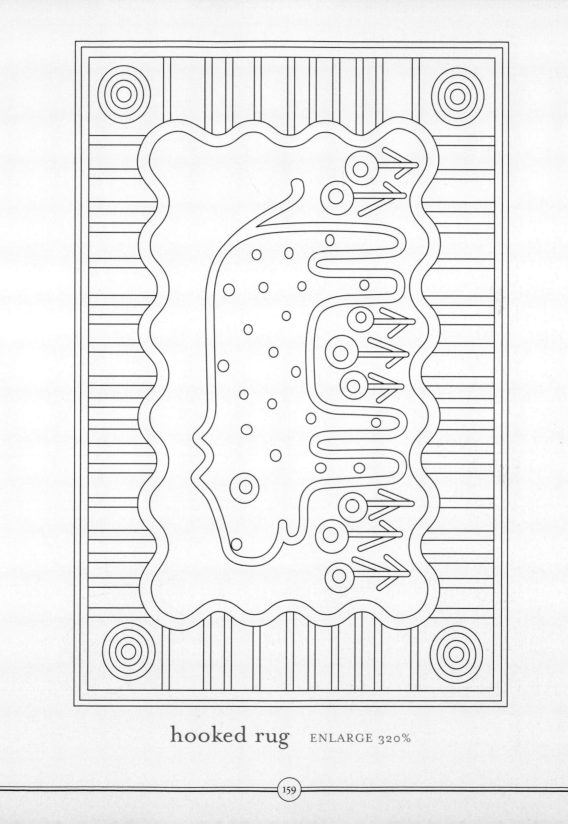

hooked rug   ENLARGE 320%

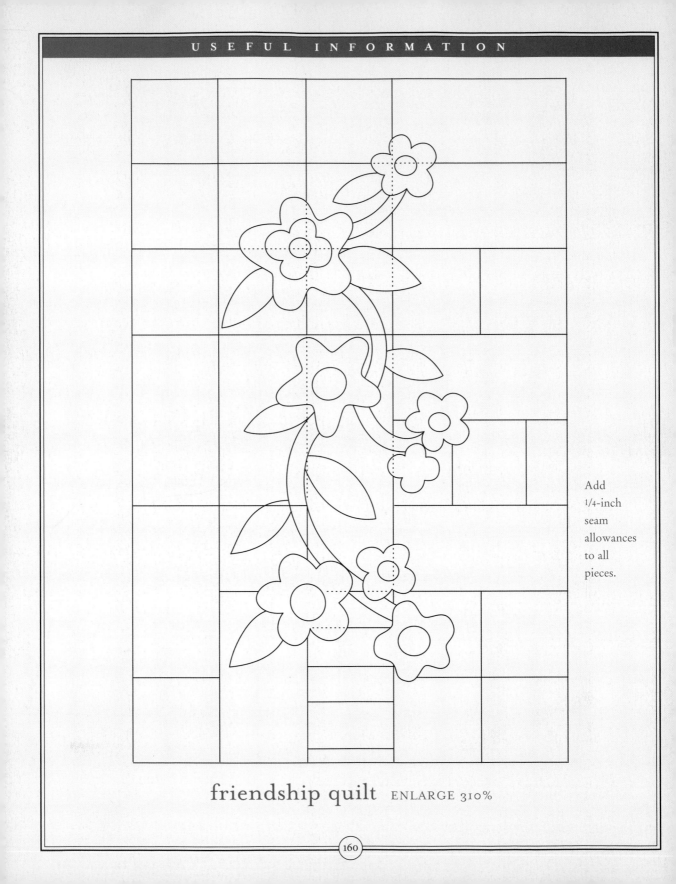

Add
1/4-inch
seam
allowances
to all
pieces.

friendship quilt ENLARGE 310%